And the S

CONVERSATIOI

A b

Alderman William Newman. J.P.
1884 - 1972.

By William V. Newman MA, BSc (Hons)

Published in 2018 by Futures Publications

Copyright © 2018 William V. Newman

British Library Cataloguing in Publication Data:
A catalogue record for this book is available
from the British Library.

ISBN-13: 978-1871131-25-5

Printed and bound by Tandem Press.

www.tandempress.com

Published in London

Dedication

I dedicate this book to my wife Jean for her great help, patience and tremendous encouragement in writing this story.

I thank our three sons, William, Michael and Mark of whom we are justly proud.

Finally, to my friends for their constant interest.

Tennyson

So flows my thought,

So runs my Dream,

That Nothing Walks with Aimless Feet,

That Not one Life shall be Destroyed,

Or Caste as Rubbish to the Void.

Introduction

I am very proud to have the privilege of editing this book by my father. I am sad that I did not finish the editing while he was still alive, as I have a lot of questions for him. This has led me to leave the editing to a minimum, I feel I need his permission to do more. I wish to leave the words to my father.

For me this book is full of stories he had told his family during his life, and at the end, bedridden with an oxygen cylinder, due to bad lungs, lying in front of the study window, looking out at the garden, birds and the trees growing on the hillside of the valley of the River Dour he was still sharing them with visitors and friends. He was laughing and proudly retelling and reliving them.

I have edited as little as possible, this has left several repetitions within a structure in which he returns to the same personalities and stories, but develops, adds or simply emphasises the importance to him. I feel this reflects his passion for telling stories and repeating them, and his pride in the friends his father made.

Dad also changes from writing in the third person as regards his father, as himself as narrator, to the first person, writing or speaking, as his father. This is partly from the fact he had tapes of interviews with his father, but also reflects his passion, and his reliving of the moments he describes. I feel, though this is grammatically and academically problematic, that it reflects how he felt in remembering, researching and writing these stories as he lay in bed. He relived his father's events. I hope therefore that the reader will join him in this reliving.

You will also notice that his memories are full of 'hot summer days'. These maybe genuine memories of the weather, or a sense of a golden childhood and past, but I feel it also reflects the view as he writes, the joy he had in living with my mum, Jean, in their wonderful home and admiring the beautiful world, through the window, he was about to leave.

This is one reason why he starts with the image of the ladybird, and with one of his poems. Jean, when looking through his letters and cards, commented on the poetry in all of them. When he was not with her, which was very rare, he would write a letter every day.

My father was a great local politician. He promoted the political career of Gwynn Prosser, helping him to become the longest serving Labour MP for Dover. Sadly, though he was involved in politics through his teacher's Union and through many discussions with the family, especially when we all listened to BBC Radio 4 'Any Questions' and BBC1's 'Question Time', he waited to near his retirement to fully engage, because of his teaching, and his dedication to his family.

As a potential academic, and lecturer, imprisoned in the job of special needs teacher, he could have been both an influential academic and a politician. His awareness of this, never expressed in public, was something that frustrated him until he remembered the value of his family and his friends.

To see him as Mayor, as Deputy Lieutenant, as Chairman, to hear his stories of the meetings, and to hear his speeches, made me proud that at last he could express his potential.

This book, in celebrating a working class man struggling to make this world, his communities, a better, more humane place, is also a tribute to Billy Newman's son, the author, and to me, and all of us who believe that human beings should respect and help each other to live in communities based on equality and justice.

I hope this set of stories will become party of the history of the communities of Eythorne, Dover, East Kent and the ongoing struggle that grandad so powerfully represents, for justice and equality, and that in some small way it will contribute and strengthen the fights we are still making

Michael Newman, Science and Citizenship teacher and Children's Rights Campaigner, November 2017

Dad sitting on his father's lap with Tilden Smith
in the grounds of his mansion.

A Portrait of the Man

Alderman William Newman. JP (Magistrate.)
Collier and Mines Inspector.

WILLIAM NEWMAN - Billy.

1884 - 1972. His Life and Times.

CONTENTS

CONVERSATIONS WITH MY FATHER.
His Life and Times. 1884 -1972.

The Beginning.

"History is a common meadow where everyone makes hay, in the manner of our living, in our giving and our taking." Part of an old Spanish proverb.

And so, to begin, not a history, not even a story, just a recollection of events from conversations with my father that have come to be so much a part of my life.

My Home is my delight. I feel the light breeze and watch the sun rise in all its morning glory.

The trees awaken, bright, and shining. The day has come.

The People stir and their eyes light up. They talk and they smile and there's friendship out there.

The People are gathering for there's work to be done. There's talk and there's laughter and games to be played. Let's all welcome in this bright new day, with its brilliant blue sky and the shine of the sun.

A ladybird lands in its curious way, most trusting, most gentle and then flies away. And so, my thoughts turn to times, not long far past, with colourful memories, some bright and some dark, all part of my world by day and by night, and so to a life, of adventure and light.

Part 1

Billy's life in Yorkshire

Chapter 1

Early recollections: Dad and his work.

My father has been described as a man who commanded much respect and attracted deep affection from people in all walks of life. They included lords and peers of the realm, bishops and military men, but those who mattered most to him were his workmates, those who worked with him, deep beneath the earth, deep below the ground. They were a particular breed of men, 'the miners'.

They worked in the dark. They were hewers of coal. Each day they would walk, from home to the pit. Each day, early, in the darkness of the morning there sounded that gathering crescendo, the tramp of feet, the pit boots heavy against the road.

The men were now gathering, a mass of shadows in the morning darkness. It was the early morning shift.

There were young, fresh faced youths, thirteen and fourteen years old, straight from school. There were old men, stocky, upright, their faces lined, pitted with black, the imprint of coal that marked their lives.

A sense of oneness pervaded the early morning, like the moistness of the rising air greeting the glimmer of a new dawn.

There was the heavy sound of pit boots and then there was silence. A sense of quiet resolution filled the air and there was silence.

Billy Newman was one of those men. He did not stand out in the crowd. He was just one of these hundreds of men. Quiet and unprepossessing, he was of physique, short and stocky, exhibiting like the others a natural strength and fitness derived from the hard nature of their work, swinging a pick for most of the day, hewing coal day after day. This was what these men, these pitmen did in the darkness of the earth, each hour of each day.

And so, it was in the 1930s. I start here, for as a young child, born in 1927, I would hear my mother and father go down stairs. It was 5 o'clock in the morning. They were up. Father was having his breakfast before going to work. It was the early-morning shift.

Mother was an excellent cook and would often make a large mince-pie. I would creep down stairs, peep through the banisters, drawn by the smell of breakfast and the thought of a slice of mince pie. But in those days, the place of the child was "to be seen, but not heard", and so satisfied with my mince pie, I would creep back off to bed.

I would not see my father again until 2 or 3 o'clock in the afternoon, when he would come home from work.

Soon after he had arrived home, he would have his dinner and then go into the room which he used as his office and have a couple of hours sleep on the settee. Mother would call him at set times. He would have arranged and ordered his day.

Father was very methodical and ensured that he used those precious moments of his time to good purpose. He would be engaged in attending to Union business, arranging meetings, meeting work folk and listening to their problems. On some days, the house would be like a doctor's surgery with four or five people seated in the other room waiting to see my father. Sometimes they sought advice on work or Union related problems, sometimes it related to more personal problems including legal advice. He had learned much concerning the law through hard experience and from consulting with his solicitor friends. If he did not know the answer to a question, he knew where to look for it.

During this time, I didn't see a great deal of my father. There was little time for home life. There was little time for family play which was left to mother, though a great time was had at Christmas and Easter festivals.

Sometimes in the summer we would go on an excursion for a day out, when a bus load of miners and their families would spend a hot summer Sunday by the sea. We would take our buckets and spades, cricket bat and balls, picnic baskets and descend from Hampshire buses onto the sands at Sandwich Bay.

These were exciting, memorable times for all the families. It was a time of getting together, of friendship and fun. The cares and concerns, the problems and worries were left behind. They were forgotten for the day. Nothing would spoil these moments of merriment.

Chapter 2

The Migration of Miners to Kent.

And so back to another day and another story.

During the 1920s and 1930s there was a great movement of people, of miners and their families from very different parts of the country. They came from the valleys of South Wales, from Somerset and Yorkshire, from the mining villages and towns all over England. The men, many unemployed, came in search of work in the newly established pits in East Kent. Tilmanstone was one of those pits, taking its name from a nearby village. They came in their hundreds not only looking for work but looking to find homes for themselves and their families.

This part of Kent was very much a rural community, sparsely populated but with small, well established, colourful country villages. Those already living here, formed close knit communities, built up over many generations. Most of the men worked on the farms and owed their living to the rich landowners. Many worked on the Lords' estates. These included the Guildford's, the Northbourne's and the Fitzwater's, whose lands took in much of this part of Kent.

Here, life appeared steady and gentle, the pace of life slow. Hay-stacks and shire-horses set the rural scene. Nature was dominant. It was harvest time. Men and women were steadily cutting the corn, bundling it into sheaves, as they made their way slowly up-field toward the setting sun.

There was however to be great change.

The miners came in their hundreds over a short period of time. They sought lodgings in the nearby coastal towns of Dover and Deal and would travel to work in the miners' buses which contractors put at the disposal of the mining company. Both Simmond's and Ayre's buses were well known to the miners in Dover. They picked up workmen from various parts of the town and took them to Tilmanstone Colliery well in time for the beginning of the early morning shift.

It was strange for many of the local population to see so many people coming to the town. They were strangers with strange accents and strange sounding voices, and they came from far and wide all in search of work. They stood out when returning home from work, black with coal dust.

These families with their different ways had come from different parts of the country and the only common bond that tied them together was their work. They were miners, part of the mining community. They were some-how different and were not welcome by many of the local people. This made the miners stick together ever more closely and form their own fraternity. The pit and everything associated with it was their life.

Chapter 3

The Model Miners' Village. 1920-1930.

Tilmanstone Pit opened in 1913 and a few houses were built at Coldred and Stonehall to provide homes for the 'Sinkers'. It was not till some years later that the new mining villages of Elvington and Aylesham and White City were built in the late 1920s and early 1930s.

Elvington, built in the late 20s, was constructed and designed as a new, model village for the miners at Tilmanstone Pit. It was a very advanced project for those particular times. An impressive group of people joined together to plan the project, and use their influence to see that the plan was implemented. They included representatives of the owners, management and the miners, Professor Abercrombie and eminent members of the existing community. Mr Tilden Smith was the moving force behind this exciting venture, where Tilmanstone miners would be housed.

Though some miners had settled in Dover, River, Whitfield, Studdal and Coldred and other surrounding villages, the majority employed at Tilmanstone Colliery moved into the houses built at Elvington.

On the left Mr Motram, Chairman of the Board of Directors, in the centre Mr Tilden Smith, owner of Tilmanstone Colliery, and to the right, Billy Newman, Union Secretary, examining houses being built at Elvington, 1927.

It was indeed a model village. Much thought was given to the design of the village. The fundamental principle that guided those in charge was that the design should reflect, as far as possible, the needs of the new village as a community, but it was made clear that such a development should not impinge in any detrimental way on the magnificence of the local countryside.

There should be a village hall and recreation ground at the heart of the community. The houses 'mostly semi-detached' would be of very good quality and design, and match any of the private houses being built at the time. They were planned to have modern bathrooms and toilets, spacious rooms and large gardens.

The facilities provided in these houses were very different from those they had left behind, which were built near the pits, often blackened with coal dust, built in crowded, narrow streets with only primitive earth toilet facilities at the bottom of the gardens. The only place for children to play was in the narrow back alleys at the bottom of their gardens.

The miners when they arrived home from work, black with coal, would have had to wash in a tin bath filled with hot water, boiled in kettles on the coal fire. In those houses there were no bathrooms. These were still the conditions that many miners and their families had to endure in many parts of the country.

As late as 1943, during my time as an evacuee in Ebbw Vale, South Wales, I lived in a house where you depended on a tin bath, in front of the fire to have a wash. There was no bathroom. Yet, some 23 years earlier, in the new village of Elvington, during the late 1920s, things were very different, the houses were built to a high standard with fully equipped bathrooms. They were built in such a way that those living in them were proud to call them home. The houses were to be situated a mile distant from the pit so that they would not be subject to coal dust. It would be a clean village.

This was their future, full of promise.

Some of the miners came individually, others came with their families and friends. There was the Welsh group, the Evans, the Jones, the Davieses and the Morgans etc; and then there were the Parfitts, the Somerset men, as well as those from Yorkshire and the North. These groups brought with them many of their own traditions, but the one thing that united them was their common experience as miners.

Chapter 4

Billy's Move to Kent. Aged 33.

Billy Newman moved from Wombwell in Yorkshire in 1917 to seek work in the newly opened coalfield in East Kent. He had read in the paper that there were vacancies for miners at Tilmanstone Colliery and that the pay and conditions there were better than those where he was working in Yorkshire and he was troubled by the increasingly tense atmosphere that pervaded the community where he lived. There had been a great deal of conflict between the management and the miners, and there was much division and quarrelling amongst the miners themselves. Added to this was the increasingly bad relations that developed between neighbours because of the terrible suffering caused by three years of war. This was not a very pleasant place to bring up a family. Billy had been happily married for twelve years, and now had four children. His first responsibility was to his family.

He wanted to go to work, receive his wages and look after his family. He did not wish to become involved with any one of the disparate factions. He had seen how the employers could sack you at any moment if you were thought to be a trouble-maker. They could blacklist you so that it would become impossible for you to get a job anywhere. Such was the nature of things where he worked in Yorkshire. It was because of such circumstances that he made one of the greatest decisions of his life which was to move away from the familiar surroundings where he had been brought up, leaving his brothers and sisters, and his friends, to search for a new life in Kent.

Billy travelled down to Dover and found temporary lodgings in Tower Hamlets. He later managed to rent a terraced house No. 14 Glenfield Road and at once sent for his family, his wife Margaret and their four children, Richard, Mary, Violet and Betty.

Billy and his wife, though excited by it all, were still very apprehensive as to what the future might hold. This was a new world. They did not know anybody. They were complete strangers in a very different part of the country. The year was 1917. It was during the time of the Great War. At this time food was in short supply and families had to queue up for their rations. Though there was conscription, miners, in 1916, were prevented from joining up because it was realised the work they did, in supplying coal, was so vital to the war effort.

Chapter 5

The Importance of Coal to the War Effort.

The importance of coal at this time needs to be made explicit. The importance of coal to the economy and to the whole way of life had not always been taken as a matter of serious concern. That it was there in plenty was taken for granted. That it was a good investment and a source of power and wealth to the owners was proven by the tight grip they maintained on the possession of their property.

However, prior to the outbreak of war in 1914, the industrialists and businessmen had turned their eyes to the treasures of Africa. They sought to exploit the rich mineral deposits of Africa. In these ventures they were supported by their governments, ambitious to extend their powers in these countries. This entailed the building up and expansion of national armies and navies. Britain prior to 1914, already had a powerful force in its Royal Navy, with Germany not far behind.

At the outbreak of the 1914 war, when the call went out to "Fight for King and Country" there was a great outbreak of patriotic fervour in all parts of the community. Miners left the pits in great numbers to join the army. Inevitably this left the pits short of man power.

Strangely, at the beginning of the war, little attention was given to the fact that the provision of coal was so vital to the war effort. It was not until 1916, two years into the war, that the government decided the pitmen must remain in the pits and that work in the mines was declared a reserved occupation.

It was at last realised that the whole industrial complex depended on coal. Without the coal factories would close and the railways would come to a halt. The ships, whether battleships or destroyers, would not be able to leave port. It was vital that the pit-men remain in the pits to use their skills and strength to dig the coal, to extract it from the depths of the Earth and thus provide this essential power which the war-machine demanded.

The great iron and steel works in the valleys of South Wales were fired up as the flames from the furnaces leapt up, reaching for the sky. Steel for the railways, steel for the ships, steel to build the machines and factories, all depended on the hot burning coal.

Coal not only provided riches and wealth to a few individuals, it powered our industries and furnished the armies and navies with a destructive power never before witnessed. This was manifest on the bloody battlefields of France in the 1914-18 war, with the tragic loss of whole generations of young men, British, French , German and Russian, Italian and Austrian and men from many other parts of the world, including the men from the Empire and America. The horror of this conflict was that it left behind scenes of destruction, desolation and bitterness on a global scale.

Chapter 6

Attendance at the Board School:
Queen Victoria and Gladstone.
Billy's Early Boyhood. Pit Boy at 13 years.
15 at the time of the Boer War.

Billy Newman would have been 30 years old when war was declared in 1914. It was against this background, times of great tragedy and disaster, that he grew up.

Born in the year 1884 during the reign of Queen Victoria, when Gladstone was Prime Minister, he was the product of the first of the Board Schools. He left school and started work at the age of 13, the year 1897.

Billy was blessed with a rich voice and a good memory and whilst at school he learned to read well. His ability to read was noted by a sympathetic teacher, who would pick him out and encourage him to read in front of the class. She taught him how to project his voice and give expression to the words he was reading and he acquired a love of language.

This Billy always remembered with much pride and he felt that it stood him in good stead later on in life and he often talked of the kindness of that teacher.

Billy was the youngest in a family of four brothers and one sister. The first borne William, died in early childhood. Jim was the eldest, followed by Dick, Jake and his sister Anne. All three brothers worked down the pit and when he left school Billy, then aged 13, was found a job in a small colliery at Tong near Bradford, where a couple of dozen or so men were employed below ground.

It was a very primitive mine where the colliers were lowered down in a large tub or would climb down on ladders built against the side of the shaft. Most of the workmen lived near each other. They knew each other as neighbours and friends.

Billy had not long been working at this pit before he came face to face with a scene that was to affect him for the rest of his life. It was imprinted deep in his memory. It was the look on the face of the twisted body of a dead man. A rock fall had hit the man whom Billy had been working with only moments before.

"No time to scream! No time to think! Just run and call for help!"

Here he was a young, fresh faced boy of 13, in his first job working in a pit, in the dark, below ground. He was working, fetching and carrying, for this man, an old and experienced collier. This man who had been alive moments ago, wielding his pick with such skill and strength, was now dead.

He, a taciturn man of few words, would now speak no more.

All had happened with an unexpected suddenness.

The big pit man who had been talking was now strangely silent. "No cry of pain! No whisper of life, just a strange dark silence with a voice of its own and the message was crawl out, quickly, quickly, hurry, hurry and find help now!"

Everything gave way to an instinctive emotional urge to move fast, regardless of any difficulty. Scraped knees and torn flesh went unnoticed in the heat of the moment. Nothing mattered except the search for help.

Those eyes, that face, he still remembered to this day. Hot, wet, sticky, imprinted on his mind. And then the men, blackened, bare-chested, hot, sweat rags, carrying the crumpled body to the pit shaft bottom before returning, through the darkness, to the work so vital to their living.

The depth of their feeling was kept hidden, but the loss of one of their comrades, their friend was a loss of great magnitude. No tears, but deeply felt, wounded, part of themselves was missing. And so once more along the tunnels into the darkness of the earth, muscles flexed, breaking rock, hewing the black coal necessary to sell, necessary to provide food for the table and pay for shelter, a place to live and provide for the family. But what of the family, the widow and three young children?

We all lived and played together. They were our friends. We were like a family, and this was how we lived. This was the year 1897.

Shortly after this terrible tragedy his brother Dick who was then 18 years old, found Billy a job at a bigger pit at Alton Main, where they could work together, but Billy still carried the bitter, sad memories of Tong with him.

Chapter 7

Dads' brother tells his Story.

A visit to Uncle Dick in Wombwell, 1945. He was in his 70s and talked of conditions at work as a young boy in the 1890s and 1900s.

Just after the end of the war, 1945, dad and I visited Dick at his home in Yorkshire. Now retired, he was still living in Wombwell where Billy had lived as a boy. They talked of old times and Uncle Dick gave a vivid description of what the life of a pit boy was like in the early 1890s. It brought back for them many memories of the kind of life they lived. Looking back they were undoubtedly hard times, but somehow they never thought about it in that way. They accepted it very much as normal. As Uncle Dick said,

"We lived it, and now, we sometimes wonder how! !"

Dick described how the pit work affected their characters at such a young age. Their father was dead and their mother was left alone to bring up the children as best as she could on very limited means. In fact she depended on the money the boys earned to keep a roof over their heads. Their mother did not want the boys to work down the pit, but there was no alternative, she needed the money.

As soon as he left school at the age of 13 Billy started work in the small mine at Tong and later moved to a large coal mine near Barnsley, where his elder brother Dick worked. Billy worked down below for 6d a day when he first started 'hurrying' -- working for one man, running tubs filled with coal from the coal-face to the collecting point where the coal was unloaded and he would push the empty tubs back to the workman at the coal-face. Sometime later after he proved he could do the job and that he was a good worker he was offered a rise in wages if he would take on two men to 'hurry for'. This he did for 6 shillings a week. They had to work eight hours a day, sometimes nine, and if they wanted you to stay an extra hour, you had to. There were no stipulated hours, "rarely did we see the light of day."

My Aunt Dinah would recall how Billy when he arrived home would often fall asleep in the room still in his "pit muck", and mother used to roll him up in her shawl and carry him to the bed.

"Many a time he'd wash next morning, and I see him with his feet out of the end of the bed and my mother picking coal out of his feet. He used to tramp that much. They were bad days and he used to have the skin torn off his back, leaving notches on his back. At finish we made him a back leather to protect him. The roof that he 'trammed' were only 18 to 20 inches high. They were running tubs and sometimes in the rush their back caught against the roof and fetched the skin off their back."

At finish Aunt Dinah and their mother made back leathers, two straps over the shoulder and two round the body. The leathers covered all of their back and so saved them from having a lot of sores, keeping their backs clean.

There were many young boys like my father who worked down the mines of this country, who for much of the year never saw the light of day. There was no time to play. There was no time to be young. No time to grow up. You were at once thrown into a man's world, and as my Uncle Dick tells it, "When we earned ten shillings a week, mother gave us two pence to spend and there were lads like us and we would take our tuppence and buy a halfpenny clay pipe and a pennyworth of tobacco. Now we could call ourselves 'Pit Lads', and well versed in the pit language we would swear and smoke. We soon learned all the pit talk. It was a hard rough life. We were accepted as 'Pit Men'."

This life continued for some time until we got work digging out the coal. We became real colliers wielding a pick, working with a group of other experienced pit men, learning skills and building up the strength necessary to last till the end of the day, and sometimes it was a long day. The year was now 1900 and Billy was 16 years of age. He had been working down the pit for the last 3 years with his brothers.

The Salvation Army.

Dick born 1879, five years older than Billy, was greatly influenced by members of the Salvation Army. He tells how when he was 16 he came home from pit one day, black as could be and found a Salvation Army lady in the house.

"I wondered what they were up to! I went into the kitchen. The kitchen door was open and I could see the captain and lieutenant in uniform kneeling down saying a prayer with my mother. They got up and the lady came into the kitchen. She held out her hand and I looked at my black hand and looked at her. She smiled and said, 'You needn't be afraid, my father's a pit man, I know what it's like. I had a brother killed in an accident at Pope-Pearsons. I know what its like!' She shook hands with me and said, 'God Bless You My Boy! Bless You!'

"Of course, she was new to me, I had nobody say anything like that before. I'd never been to a Sunday School and of course, I knew nothing about religion. I was struck with her manner and my curiosity was roused. What was there to this religion where people dressed up in uniform and were willing to go visiting the likes of us and say prayers with us? The lady said, 'Your mother's coming to the Salvation Army meeting on Sunday night. Will you come with her?' And so I went.

"The meeting was held in a big old wool shed and people came from all over. The room was packed to the doors. I got down on a back seat, stopped there and listened to what was said. Of course I didn't understand all that was said, but something came over me! I felt there must be something good, and I felt I wanted to be better and lead a better life. These people had something to offer and I was willing to take it. I was willing to learn. I worked my way to the front and the Captain shook me by the hand and said, 'Will you come to Jesus?' I said 'Yes, I will!' and I went and knelt down. Well, I didn't know what to say. I'd never been taught anything like this before, but it were in my mind that I could be something better, so I knelt down and prayed in my way. I said, 'Help me Lord to be a better lad! Help me to give up cussing and swearing so that I can live a better life!' "

Dick remained a strong Salvationist all his life. His three sons all learned musical instruments and became Salvation Army band masters. Dick's life style affected the family. Billy, his younger brother, was a little sceptical and felt that Dick may have been greatly influenced in his conversion by the nature of the organisation and the religious service. The persons conducting the service were dressed in uniform which gave them an air of authority and they spoke, when preaching, with confidence, a manner which imparted a feeling of certainty.

Then there was the effect of being in a large crowd and the possibility of being carried along by the emotions of the crowd. This emotive atmosphere was strengthened by the manner in which crowd participation was encouraged, in the kind of responses suggested by the platform. They appealed to deep feelings of the congregation which were difficult to resist.

Billy may have attended such meetings when he was older. The Salvation Army had quite a large following in that part of Yorkshire. People who were not members of the Salvation Army still had great respect for it. However Billy remained a little sceptical, and went his separate way.

This period was a time of great political and religious ferment. It was at the time when people of good-will were very much concerned with the growing state of poverty in parts of our cities, particularly in London's East End.

William Booth, (1829-1912), founder of the Salvation Army, was first a methodist minister and it was in 1865 he organised his own religious group of workers among London's poor. His Christian mission in the East End of London became the Salvation Army in 1880 and his remarkable book, 'Darkest England and the Way Out!', was well received by many of the intellectual class. This owed much to his diligent research and the factual evidence that he provided.

The work of William Booth and his devoted group of workers in the East End of London gave great impetus to the growth of the Salvation Army. It caught the attention of the likes of Bernard Shaw as depicted in his famous play 'Major Barbara', which still appears on the London stage some 50 or more years later.

Jack Lawson confirms, in an essay in the book 'The Discovery of Sidney Webb', the conditions described by my Uncle Dick under which they worked. He gives a most vivid account of work in the coal mines of the 1890s and the early 1900s. He writes,

"The work two thousand feet below ground did not bother us much. It became a matter of habit. Naked, balled up between a pony and a small truck, which sometimes weighed a ton when filled with coal, we raced along narrow, dark roadways. Now and then the truck struck a joint in the rail and over she went, coal smashing over you, often leaving you marked for the rest of your life. Or as a 'Coal Hewer' at the face, we doubled ourselves up in very low places, sweating, and squirming, wielding the pick, getting the coal. There was no minimum wage. If you were lucky you took home enough to pay the grocer and the butcher.

"We didn't mind the conditions, we didn't mind the contorting, sweaty, dangerous work, it was the demand for reductions of wages that made us so angry."

Did anyone consider how they would pay for a room over their heads? Did anyone care?

The Miners Federation was little more than a name. Loyalties were very much local, with the workmen they knew, with the people they lived with, their friends and neighbours. There were many quarrels and arguments between the different factions. Different groups were played off one against another. This situation was made worse by the use of the 'Butty System', a method of employment and payment used in most pits. It was a pernicious system, which many of the miners fought long and hard to eradicate. In many of the men's minds there remained only the bitter band of unforgettable memories, the hardships and the struggles, the strikes that deeply affected their lives.

Chapter 8

Europe turns to Empire and Africa in Search for Raw Materials.

As a young 16 year old in 1900, at the turn of the century, Billy would have heard tales of the wars in South Africa, the Boer War, Baden-Powell, the Zulus and the Dutch settlers. The Jameson Raid and the battle at Mafeking were all stories of a great patriotic War. This was still a time of Empire, of exploration and the search for territory and conquest, particularly in Africa.

There was a search for the possession of territories that were rich in raw materials, raw materials that were necessary to feed our factories, our industries back home. Other European countries were embarked on the same mission. The Dutch went into South Africa, the Belgians and French invaded the Congo, and the Germans sent troops to parts of central Africa.

People from all walks of life were touched by this spirit of King and country, of Empire. Kipling and Baden-Powell became emblems representing the spirit of the time. Even Bernard Shaw spoke sympathetically in favour of Empire, and he, a founder-member of the Fabian Society.

The miners, though influenced by what was happening in the world, were more concerned with their own immediate problems. For many of the wealthier people in the country, the period following the Boer War was one of peace and prosperity.

However, the situation of the miners did not change. The owners still demanded that there must be cuts in wages. The attitude of most people in authority was sympathetic to the mine owners. The pit men were still regarded as a people apart, of the lowest class, a menial folk. They were the undeserving section of the population.

Chapter 9

Pit Disasters 1908-1913 and the General Public.

But something was to happen which focussed full public attention on the miners' plight. A series of great disasters occurred when human life was destroyed on a scale and with a suddenness unparalleled in the history of British coal mining. They all happened within the space of 5 years, 1908 to 1913. The disasters occurred on such a massive scale that the public could not fail to ignore such tragedy with its consequent suffering in the mining community.

In 1908, the Maypole Pit in Lancashire set on fire with a loss of 76 lives. In 1909, West Stanley Pit exploded with an even greater loss of life, 168 in total. And then in 1910 the Hulton Pit fire with a loss of 344 lives, and in that same year there was an explosion at Whitehaven where 136 miners died. In 1912 there occurred the Cadeby Main disaster in Yorkshire with the loss of 85 men. But the worst was yet to come in 1913 in North Wales at Senghenydd Pit, where explosions caused the death of 440 men.

A cumulative series of tragedies of vast proportion had taken place in which young men in the prime of their lives, fathers and sons, men living along the same road, whole communities were decimated. This was a period of tragedy beyond imagining. It brought to public attention a group of work people who had for so long been ignored. The public were forced to pay attention to the dangerous conditions under which the miners worked. They were told of the poor conditions in which the families lived.

For those working in the pits, the affect was of deep personal tragedy. Miners wives stood and watched as they saw their men off to work, wondering if they would return home!

These disasters were by no means the only ones that occurred or even the most tragic. During the course of mining history there had been many disasters. The problems encountered deep below ground, the dangers of flooding and explosions caused by the accumulation of gas, which the slightest spark of a pick could set off, were almost taken for granted. Safety was a secondary consideration.

The first concern of the miner was his pay packet. Would he have enough money to pay for his living! How much money would he take home at the end of the week. And the prime consideration of the owners was, "How much money would they make? What would their profit be?" This lead to far too many cases of negligence resulting in accidents and deep suffering.

The owners and the miners regarded each other as very different kinds of people. They lived in different worlds. They were divided in terms of wealth. The owners were rich. They lived in big houses, mansions in the country-side, away from the dirt and grime of the pits. They lived with people of similar status and felt themselves mentally superior. They were a class apart.

An article in the newspaper, The Guardian, by Michael Parkin, page 7, entitled 'EXPLOSION', commemorates the great tragedy that occurred at Oakes Colliery over a hundred years ago, December 1866. This was some twenty years before Billy was born, but it was still talked of during Billy's time when he worked in pits near Barnsley where it happened.

A series of explosions at Oakes Colliery, Barnsley, killed 360 men and boys and drove rescuers to the heights of heroism. It was England's worst colliery disaster: "The rescuers still have their monument, a soulful bronze angel humping a half-naked man, on the Doncaster road..."

The Oakes Colliery exploded at 1.20 pm on December 12th, hurling smoke and wreckage up the 900-foot shaft - like a suddenly agitated volcano. The first men brought up were hideously burned. Rescuers went through the galleries to find the bodies: boys aged 11 and 12, fathers clutching their sons, 38 dead men gassed by choke damp and lying still with their arms entwined, just as they had stumbled towards the pit bottom and safety.

All but six of the 340 miners in the pit died in that first explosion. Parkin Jeffcock, a mining engineer, was leading a rescue team of 26 men the following day when the pit was once again rocked by an explosion. There was silence until the next day when men on the surface heard a sound from the bottom of the shaft. They lowered a rope with a bottle of brandy attached, and the bottle was removed with Barnsley alacrity. Descending nearly 900 feet in a bucket, through clouds of smoke, to the bottom of the burning pit, John Mammatt and Thomas Embleton found the sole survivor of Jeffcock's rescue team and brought him to the surface.

Many Oakes Colliery victims were buried in a mass grave at Barnsley cemetery, buried without a memorial. Some 100 or more bodies are still entombed in the sealed pit, which serves as a reminder of the tremendous suffering of those families and the wrecking of a whole community.

A public meeting was called to open a relief fund. The platform included the Archbishop of York, and Earl Fitzwilliam, the Lord Lieutenant of West Riding, Viscount Halifax, Lord Wharncliffe and Viscount Milton together with a number of MPs and clergy, but their words rang hollow when they expressed sympathy for the owners at their great loss of property at the same time as expressing sympathy for the families of the dead, such was the reverence for the sanctity of property. This attitude, equating the working class as undeserving, something less than human, was best expressed many years later by J. B. Priestly in his famous play 'An Inspector Calls'.

Though the plight of the miners had been brought to public attention by the series of disasters that occurred between 1908 and 1913, during which time some 1,249 miners were killed, little had changed in the relationship between the owners and the workmen.

It was in these times of immense tragedy and momentous events that Billy Newman spent his youth. They happened and affected him and his family deeply, during his most formative years. He worked in the pit near Barnsley. The people he worked with were part of his life. He talked with other miners and listened to their stories. He read the local papers and studied the numerous pamphlets printed by the various political factions, mostly left wing and groups of dissenters, critics of that period.

The Salvation Army
Branches of the Salvation Army had become well established in Billy's home town of Wombwell. The members in their smart uniforms were very active in the neighbourhood. Their influence was widely felt. Billy had great admiration for the work they did, particularly amongst the poor and the needy. He would attend services with his mother and brother and enjoyed listening to the brass band but he was not attracted by the uniform which he thought too militaristic. This was a time soon after the Boer War. Billy felt that this war in South Africa was very much one of conquest, of colonization and exploitation. It was not a mission which could in anyway be described as a 'Just War'. Billy could never support such actions.

Chapter 10

Aged 16-19. A Young Mans' Thoughts turn to Fun and Romance.

It was 1900, it was the turn of the century and Billy was 16 years old. His life was taken up with work and he had little spare time. There was not much time to play. Thoughts of political and social problems were not uppermost in his mind. He, like most other young men, was more concerned with going out and having fun on a Saturday night, of going to dances and socials organised by the local churches and chapels, of meeting young ladies and chasing after the girls with his brother Jake. They were the youngest in the family.

Sometimes coach trips would be organised with visits to Blackpool, Robin Hood Bay, and Scarborough. At other times, the fair would visit the town and all the local young folk would be there, taking turns on the coconut shies or tugging the ropes in the swinging boats. They were places of getting to know other young people, of laughter and fun.

It was on such a day out on a coach outing to Robin Hood Bay that Billy met Margaret Neale who became the love of his life. At the age of 22 they were married at a church in Thornton. They rented some rooms in Wombwell where the rest of his family lived. Margaret was one of the 'Mill Girls'. She had worked in the mill from her early school days. She would have been 8 or 9 years of age and this had been her life for as long as she could remember. Margaret continued working in the mill until she had a family. A year soon after they were married, Richard was born. This would be in the year 1907, a year before the great pit disaster of 1908.

Billy, a young man of 21, devoted all his time and thoughts to looking after his family. Like most other young men he had that romantic spirit and was full of optimism. He had dreams and hopes and he was very much in love with Margaret. All other concerns receded into the background. Such concerns were still there, but existed as shadows in the recesses of his mind. His home, his family came first. In spite of having very little, they were very happy, wrapped up in a world of their own. It was a place which was their paradise. It was their world.

They were fortunate to have two rooms, a bedroom and kitchen come dining room. They had very little furniture. Their sleeping facilities consisted of mattresses on the floor and in the other room just a bare table and three wooden chairs. They had to share the cooking stove and obtain hot water boiled over the fire, from the people downstairs.

There was no bathroom. They, like most other working class families at that time, used a tin bath which they filled with water heated in kettles on the coal fire.

The toilets were earth lavatories at the bottom of the very small gardens. The houses had been built very close to one another. They were terraced houses and the rows of houses backed on to one another. A narrow lane divided one row from another. There was not much room for privacy. It was a crowded space. There was little room for the children to play.

In the centre are Margaret, 23, and Billy Newman, 22,
on their wedding day at Thornton Church,
with his brothers Jim and Dick and their wives.

There was a great deal of hardship, but the women, like their men in the pits, worked together and would help one another. In many cases common problems, common troubles were shared and friendships were established. A sense of comradeship grew up between the families.

Billy, now married, was no longer like his brother Jake, the man about town. He now had responsibilities which he took very seriously. This was to him a new life. He would work hard to ensure he would take home enough money to provide for his family.

Chapter 11

Politics and the Union.

As time went by, Billy came to have strong views on the political and social issues. He was an avid reader, endowed with a good memory. He read the political pamphlets that were available, and often spoke of Blatchford's 'Clarion'. He listened to stories of Victor Grayson, the young eloquent, fiery spokesman who was elected as a Socialist Member of Parliament, in spite of the fact that the Labour Party refused to endorse his candidature, and would not support him. He fought on a programme of uncompromising socialism. This took place in the year 1908 in a sensational by-election in the Colne Valley. He became a legend in his time. Some years later, whilst still a Member of Parliament, he walked out of a West End hotel and was never heard of or seen again. His disappearance still remains a mystery today.

Billy Newman would then have been 24 years old.

There were names such as Phillip Snowden, Keir Hardie, Bob Smillie, all well-known names among the political activists still dependent on the support of the Liberal Party. The Socialist Democratic Federation and the ILP, the Independent Labour Party, with the support of the eloquent Jimmy Maxton, grew in strength and began to be the organisations that represented the labour and trade union movements.

The recent tragic disasters in the pits at that time affected him greatly. Then there was the great struggle for shorter hours, the campaign for the eight-hour day. These workmen wanted to see the light of the day.

"As early as 1891, in the nearby Durham Coalfield, the Durham miners had secured a local agreement with the owners, granting the hewers of coal a 7 hour day. This placed the Durham miners a quarter of a century in advance of any other coalfield. It was not until 1908 that parliament enacted legislation that the maximum hours below ground should be 8 hours, in addition to one winding time and as a result, a two-shift system was adopted in many of the mines. Before this most mines worked one shift of 12 hours or more. Many workers never saw the light of day." ('The Story of the Durham Miners', by Sidney Webb. Page 69.)

All this was happening during Billy's youth . He would have been 24 when the 1908 act was passed. He had been working down the pits since he was a boy of 13 which was in the year 1897 and had worked through these times of such turbulent activities.

Billy was well aware of these struggles, and the concerns of his fellow workers. He was well aware of the deep feelings engendered as a result of the hardships experienced. However his family came first. He knew of the power of the owners. He knew the manner in which the Managers acted on behalf of the owners. He felt that sense of insecurity of employment. This was not because of a lack of work. this was because of the power of the boss over the workman. You could easily be labelled a 'Trouble Maker' and your job put at risk and even sacked and blacklisted, which would make it impossible for you to get work elsewhere. With such thoughts at the back of his mind, in spite of his feelings and his very strong political opinions, he was determined to keep out of trouble.

During this time between 1907 and 1916 Margaret had four children, Richard, Mary, Violet and Elizabeth. They had few luxuries and little money to spend. They would enjoy walks through the countryside, visit their friends and relatives, attend open air meetings, and the services and socials held by the local Salvation Army. They lead a frugal life, but for them it was a happy time. In spite of all that was happening in the world, with all its uncertainties, they enjoyed what they could and Billy took a positive outlook.

Billy and Margaret's family 1907 – 1916
The four children; Mary, Elizabeth, Richard, and Violet.

Chapter 12

Technical Innovations and the 1914 War.

A mood of change was in the air. Innovation was on the march. The motor car had made its advent and railways were now a common feature of the landscape. Bleriot had flown the Channel and in Germany and England they were experimenting with airships. This was a period of great change. The factories and industrial buildings were in full throttle. Iron and steel production increased, supplying demand from abroad, particularly in countries building railways, such as South America and Africa. Many firms such as Vickers Armstrong in England, the Bethlehem Steel Corporation of America, Krupps and Thyssen in Germany and Le Creusot in France were all increasing their production of armaments. Steel was in great demand and coal was needed to supply the furnaces. Shipyards were engaged in the production of naval vessels as well as passenger ships.

In spite of this there was little thought of danger. There was no talk of war. People were too engrossed in their own well-being to give any thought as to what was happening on the international scene. Thus what occurred in 1914 came suddenly, a complete shock to the system. A new era had suddenly sprung itself on the people of this country. It was an era which would fundamentally affect the people's attitudes and behaviour for many years to come.

It was a beautiful summer. People were determined to enjoy their Bank Holiday, so much so that when they returned home, they were surprised to learn that a state of war existed between Britain and Germany, a war which would lead to the bloodiest conflict history had ever witnessed. It was tragic in its enormity, in its killing and in the nature of the suffering wrought upon humanity on such a massive scale.

The Great War 1914.
Britain had a small volunteer army facing the might of a large German military force. Many more soldiers would be needed if the British Army was to be effective.

Soon after the outbreak of war various policies were embarked upon by the government to increase the number of volunteer soldiers and so started a vast poster campaign with the patriotic call "Your Country Needs You!" The well-known stars of the theatre and music halls sang songs to the crowded audiences. They became popular overnight and were repeated in all the concert halls and pubs around the country.

A patriotic fervour spread throughout the land. Young men rushed to join up. Families with one son or more would go off together with their friends joining the same regiment. The army gave the names of towns to many regiments and they became known as the 'Pals Regiments'. Though it proved effective in increasing the number of volunteers coming forward, this policy produced some less than beneficial effects, which became obvious, later on in the war.

Many of the early volunteers taken up with this patriotic surge were the coal miners. They later became a valued resource in carrying out the strategy and tactics adopted early on in the course of the war, notably trench warfare and the digging of tunnels below the enemy positions where huge powerful explosives were placed, and when exploded caused great damage.

As the war progressed the pits became seriously short of workers. The government found itself in an awkward situation, with the conflicting demands of manpower for the military and manpower for the mines.

Coal was urgently needed to power the factories that produced the guns and shells so vital to the war effort. Without coal the Royal Navy would not be able to send its ships to sea. Eventually in 1916, some two years after war had been declared, mining was made a reserved occupation. Pitmen became exempt from serving with the forces, they had to continue working down the pits supplying the coal that the country so urgently needed. However this policy was not without serious consequences for many of those men who remained behind in their home towns.

In 1916 a great offensive was set in motion on the British Front in which tens of thousands of troops were deployed. Wave after wave of infantry soldiers climbed out from the comparative safety of the trenches into the open spaces of no-man's land. They crossed open land marked by shell holes, muddied by the rain and sometimes filled with water. The troops marched upright with their rifles at the ready in support of each other. They were clearly visible to the German soldiers who after sheltering in their dug-outs during the artillery bombardment were now at the ready, manning their deadly machine guns.

The British troops walking wave after wave provided easy targets as the bullets from the German machine guns did their deadly work. Men were killed in their tens, then their hundreds and then within a few hours, their thousands.

The Battle of the Somme was one of the great offensives of the war. It began on that early morning of July 1st and continued until the end of November. The total British losses in this great battle were close on 500,000 men. It was slaughter on a cruel and massive scale. Such sacrifices of men had never been experienced or dreamed of before. It was warfare, killing on a scale beyond imagination. The effect of such vast numbers of men dead, killed in action, had deep and diverse affects on the people back home.

The men who had joined the volunteer army when called upon to defend their country came from the same villages, the same towns. They joined together, served with each other, members of the same family, friends and neighbours. These men had grown up together, played and worked together, and now they fought and faced these terrible dangers together. When enemy shells exploded near their trench and enemy machine guns opened fire they died together.

Telegrams in buff coloured envelopes, and sometimes with a letter from an officer, would arrive through the door announcing the death of a loved one, killed in action. During the Battle of the Somme such letters would arrive not just at one house but at several in the same street. Notices would appear in the local and national newspapers. Names were placed on the local notice-board. The whole neighbourhood would gather together to see whether any of their relatives or friends were amongst those names.

Feelings ran high and expressions of grief and anguish often turned to feelings of anger and hatred.

The feelings of sadness were mixed with questions of was it all worth it. The country had been filled with hopes of a short victorious war, that their men would return home, heroes, having done great deeds defending their country, feted and cheered by all as they proudly marched through the town. Such hopes were dashed by the heartache caused when that feared, that hated, buff envelope was delivered by the postman.

Reserved Occupation 1916.
During this time many men, mostly the older men, were still working and living at home. A number of others were in reserved occupations. The nature of their work was considered extremely vital to the war effort. Coal-mining was one such occupation.

In the early years of the war, taken up with the national spirit of patriotism which swept the country, the miners, the pitmen rushed to join the army. They responded to the call of Lord Kitchener, "Your King and Country Needs you!" They would defend their country. They would fight for Britannia.

One of the consequences resulting from this patriotic rush was that the mines became short of labour. Coal was vital to the war effort. The demand for coal was outstripping supply. More coal was needed, and so mining was at last declared a reserved occupation. Miners were no longer allowed to leave the mines to join the armed forces. For a time this position was received without any particular feelings being aroused. It was taken as normal. The miners in the neighbourhood were treated, as always, as neighbours and friends. But when during the Battle of the Somme, letters were received of love ones killed in action, attitudes changed. "Why should their men die while others in the street live safely at home?"

Friendly attitudes changed to expressions of bitterness toward the men who remained at home. This bitterness was more and more directed towards the wives and families.

Gone was that cheerful greeting, the friendly chat, the smiles of those passing on the street. Friendships broke up and in some cases neighbour was set against neighbour. It even affected relations between the children. Mothers stopped their children playing with those where the men had not gone to war.

Life amongst some of those working in the pits became difficult especially where it affected the family. The younger men were given white feathers and accused of cowardice. White feathers were given directly to the men, but in some cases they were presented to their wives, often in public places to maximum effect. It was in such an atmosphere that Billy Newman and his family found themselves. He was deeply affected by all this when he found a notice in a national newspaper advertising work in the new Kent coalfield.

Part 2

Billy moves to Kent

Chapter 13

Move to Glenfield Road, Dover, Kent. 1917.

He was very attracted to the prospect of moving to the beautiful coast of Kent especially when he read that the wages in the Kent mines were slightly higher than those he was receiving in Yorkshire. In his mind such an opportunity offered the possibility of a new start, a new life. It would be a great relief to move away from the troublesome atmosphere he and his family had to endure in their present situation. The prospects of such a proposition greatly appealed to Billy Newman. He talked it over with Margaret, his wife, and they came to a joint decision that he should take a chance and apply for work at Tilmanstone Colliery near Dover, Kent.

This was one of the biggest decisions of his life. The family had never travelled further than Blackpool. The towns they had visited included Scarborough and the sea-side resort of Robin Hood Bay. They had never been to London or Dover. They were about to embark on a completely new and great adventure.

His application having been acknowledged, Billy journeyed down to Dover and found lodgings in a house in Tower Hamlets. He then went to the pit to secure a job and information on when he could start. During the course of the following weeks he busied himself looking for a place to rent, one large enough for his family. Such a place he was fortunate enough to find at 14 Glenfield Road, Dover. It was a small, terraced house. To him it was a paradise. Not only were there more rooms, but it had a good back-garden, a place where the children might play, and there was space enough for mother to hang out the washing. The air was fresh and clear and there was no danger of coal dust covering everything, this was idyllic.

Within weeks the family had moved in. Their new life had begun. The children registered at the local elementary school at Buckland. Mother, a friendly, sociable north country woman, soon made contact with her neighbours, one of whom became a close and most helpful friend, a Mrs Collins who worked at the Co-op Library.

The year was 1917. The war was at its height and food was short but they managed to get by, and sometimes they would treat themselves by going to the local chip shop and taking home sufficient food for supper.

It is recorded that at times the rumble of gunfire from the great artillery barrages on the Western Front in France could be heard in Dover and along the south-east coast. Warships filled the harbour, all part of the famous Dover Patrol commanded by Sir Roger Keyes. Mother told me stories of the scuttling of the Glatton full of explosives, the raid on Zeebruge and HMS Vindictive, but perhaps the most exciting story was that which concerned the exploits of 'Evans of the Broke'. Troops could be seen about the town awaiting embarkation for France. Dover was indeed an important military and naval Town. At night time the sky was lit up by search lights, on the lookout for the huge German Zeppelins, carrying their deadly load of explosives to drop on London.

Father said that sometimes when taking an evening stroll on the heights of Old Park they would see such airships slowly passing overhead. Such sights he had never seen before. They brought the thoughts of war closer to home, but somehow they were thoughts and experiences they all had to live with. These were tragic times that affected everybody.

In an effort to help supply the family with enough food Billy shared an allotment with a neighbour and kept a few chickens in the back garden to supply the family with some fresh eggs, but most of his time was spent at work at Tilmanstone in the pit, a thousand feet or more below ground, hewing coal.

Chapter 14

Work at Tilmanstone. 1917 - 39.
Tilden Smith. Dean of Canterbury, Dr. Bell.
Brigadier Sir Wyndham Deedes. The Settlement Wardens.

First Days at Tilmanstone Colliery 1917.
"I well remember those first few days. I started work at
Tilmanstone Colliery. It was the early morning shift. I had
obtained an old second hand bicycle, which became a useful
means of transport. Getting up at five o-clock in the morning,
having a quick breakfast which my wife had prepared for me
and taking sandwiches, bread and dripping and a flask of tea
for 'snap', I was soon off, pedalling through the darkness of
the night with the aid of my carbide cycle lamp. Five miles to
go. Must be there in good time to collect my pit lamp before
the start of the early morning shift.

"The air was cool and fresh. The narrow country lanes were
quiet and deserted. The only sight was the dark shadowy
outline of the trees and fields, and as the dawn began to break
I felt a sense of excitement countering that feeling of
apprehension at the thought of meeting and working with men
who were strangers to me.

"The first fortnight seemed to fly by. It was a time of getting
to know my workmates and the routines of the workplace. The
men formed a close knit group and took their time before they
would fully accept a newcomer. The lights of the lamp cabin
were on signalling that the early morning shift was about to
start. The men gathered together to collect their pit lamps. It
was a meeting place where the men joined together with their
workmates giving a feeling of closeness, a sense of solidarity and
security before walking across the pit top to enter the cage. The
doors closed and the great wheel began to turn. The cage moved
into the black hole. It gathered speed and raced downwards, and
then with a brief suddenness came to a halt. The doors opened
and we all filed out into the dimly lit tunnel at the start of our
walk to the place of work. Sometimes a very long walk.

"During those first weeks the atmosphere was good. The men whom I worked with became more open in their attitude and I began to feel I was a real part of the team. I no longer felt an outsider. We were a mixed bunch, two from Somerset and two from South Wales and myself a Yorkshire-man.

"I was filled with a sense of optimism. Everything seemed to be going well. I had a regular job, a sure wage, and though the amount was small, it was money in my pocket and I could support my family.

"As I cycled that afternoon through the sunlit Kent countryside, with the fields of golden corn stretching as far as the eye could see, I was going home, home to see my family and I felt nothing could go wrong. All was well with the world"

Chapter 15

Billy did not want to join the Union.

Billy had a job. At the end of the week he took home a wage. They had a nice home and were making friends. Mother managed to obtain an old knitting machine on which she made socks and scarves, which she would sell to supplement father's income.

Dover was a very attractive town. The one thing they wanted to be sure of was security. They wanted to know that their good fortune would last. Bearing in mind the experiences they had been through in Yorkshire, they came to a decision, that Billy should stay out of the Union. He did not wish to give his new employers the impression that he was a trouble-maker. He knew how easy it was for the management to give you the sack. He had seen some of his friends being blacklisted, making it difficult, if not impossible to get a job elsewhere. He was determined to avoid any such situation now or in the future. He would keep clear of trouble.

"I had made up my mind to stick to my work and earn a living, to serve my family and enjoy myself with my wife and children at the sea-side. I felt it was a man's right to work and to be at peace within the circle of a happy family. It would be the fulfilment of a dream, to walk in the green fields and to walk along the sea-shore and hear the roar of the surf, and in the warm summer evening twilight, hear the hushed murmur of the sea. The children would laugh and smile with delight, and big eyed, convey a sense of curious wondering .

"It was with such thoughts in my mind that some weeks later I set off to work. It was a Friday, pay day. I had been working underground for some weeks at Tilmanstone Colliery, and had built up a friendly relationship with the group of miners with whom I worked. I began to feel secure and confident, but fate moves in mysterious ways. Things can change with unexpected suddenness. No warning signals! No moment for reflection! The lightning struck!

"As part of my work I had been laying 'Flat Sheets' and in Yorkshire we had been paid at a special rate in addition to our normal wages. That Friday afternoon I examined my pay packet as I crossed the pit top and found that this amount was not included in my wages. I was puzzled. There must be some mistake?

"Being somewhat reticent about going directly to the office with my complaint, I stood and waited. What should I do? I was a newcomer and did not want to be misunderstood or looked upon as a trouble maker. It was then I noticed a deputy coming across the pit top. I saw he had just come out of the office. I thought he might be able and willing to give me some advice. I approached him and dutifully took off my cap, rolled it in my hand and somewhat nervously confronted him.

"He stopped and looked at me with a strange inquisitorial gaze. He just waited. There was no word just a questioning gaze! I felt embarrassed and struggled for the correct words. I found my voice and expressed my concerns as best I could. I was polite in my manner and waited for an answer. I had hoped for some advice, some wise counsel. This was not to be. His reaction was, to say the least, somewhat abrupt! Most would have judged his manner as downright rude. How dare I accost him on the pit top! It was none of his business! My pay packet must be correct! 'Go and see your Trade Union representative. It's not my problem!' I grew angry and started to question him further. However feeling that I might get myself in deep trouble, I curbed my anger and swallowed my pride, apologised and went on my way.

"Some of the men, who were standing nearby and had heard the somewhat heated part of the confrontation, came up to me and asked if I would be going to the Union meeting on Sunday morning. My reply was no! I was a newcomer and did not want to become known as a 'trouble maker'. I did not want to endanger my position. I needed this work to feed my family. No! I would not go to the Union meeting, but I would see the Union representative and seek his advice. This I did and all he told me was that I should go down to the colliery offices and take it up with the management. He was a complacent individual.

"It is sometimes surprising how what may appear to be a small incident at the time can have such a major effect on a person's life. Each morning I set out for work at the pit. Each morning I closed my mind to the concerns that anything would change. I hoped and believed that the good relations I had built up with my fellow workmates would continue and all would be for the best. Such, I soon discovered, was not to be. If I believed this, I soon found out I was living in a dream world.

"At first nothing seemed to change except that each morning at work I would be asked by one of the pit-men that same question, 'Are you coming to the Union meeting Billy? You really laid into that Deputy the other day and good for you!'

"'Thanks for the invite but my answer is still No!'

"Sunday passed and I noticed, each day, the attitude of my workmates began to change. Gone was the cheery laughter, gone was the friendly banter. The general atmosphere was cold and conversation stopped when I approached. Some of the men openly avoided me. Others would come close and in passing would make comments that 'He is all mouth but he hasn't got the guts to do anything!' I felt isolated. I had become an unwanted stranger and when I got up in the morning even the thought of going to work had become unbearable.

"Realising the situation would not change I talked to my wife about the circumstances I found myself in, and the affect it was having on me. She became very worried and said that I shouldn't allow it to go on like this and that it might be better if I joined with the men and attended the next Union meeting.

"It would be worthwhile if it meant that the people you work with become friendly once more. 'You can't go to work especially in places of danger, where you work so closely together and depend so much on each other, so, Yes! join the Union.' Thus the decision was made and a new situation arose which was profoundly to affect the rest of my life and that of my family. I joined the Union. It was 1917."

Chapter 16

War weariness and Times of Unrest Throughout the Country.

"The year was 1917 and I was 33 years old. It was during the time of the Great War and still there seemed no end, just a time of endless slaughter; loved ones dying for a few yards of ground. Young men, the flower of the nation, injured and dead in 'No-Man's Land'."

There was now spreading a feeling of war weariness and disillusion. Unrest broke out in some parts of the country. There were even strikes in some industries, men refusing to work. However, the national spirit of support for the war was still there. The notion of duty in the fight for 'King and country' still remained deep within the consciousness of the mass of the people and so the war, with all its consequences, dragged on.

"I was an avid reader and interested in thoughts and actions that affected the people and the workers. Though up to this time not active in politics, I kept myself well informed. I was attracted by past events, reading about the Peasants Revolt, the Chartists and the epic struggles of the agricultural labourers at Tilsbury and Tolpuddle. I knew of the Webbs and Bernard Shaw and the Fabian Movement. There were the great names of the Miners Federation in Durham and Yorkshire in the early 1900s, Bob Smilli, and Keir Hardie in the Liberal then the Labour movement, champions of the workers. We were enthused by the articles in Blatchford's 'Clarion' and other progressive writings...

"Then there was the epic campaign of Victor Grayson who stood on a socialist Programme, in spite of opposition of those said to be the official representatives of Labour, including Phillip Snowden. Grayson won the seat and became M.P. for Colne Valley in Durham. Only 25, a brilliant speaker who drew the crowds with his words. Such were the experiences and times of my early youth. They were embedded in my thoughts and my mind. They were more than memories; they were my life.

"It was this background of knowledge that stood me in good stead in the changed situation in which I was to find myself. I came to have a good knowledge of the nitty gritty, the everyday substance of politics, though even with all the knowledge I had accumulated I found there was always a surprise just around the corner".

Attendance at Union.

"It was in the summer of 1917, the month August, when I first started work at Tilmanstone Colliery. I remember it well for it was a delightfully warm summer. All was bright in the countryside. It was a wonderful time to bring the family down to live in such a magnificent setting.

"There were the rolling hills of the Downs on one side and on the other the sea, sparkling in the sunlight. The scene was a joy to behold. But this feeling of well-being was short lived. The troubles I encountered at work amongst my fellow workers affected me deeply. They were such that all my cherished hopes for the future would be dashed. It was because of these circumstances that I felt I must change my position.

"I was still apprehensive about joining the Union but felt I had no alternative if I wanted to have the respect and friendship of the men with whom I worked. It was in this state of mind that some weeks later I attended my first Union meeting.

"I was not particularly enthusiastic. I wondered how I would be received after all that had gone before..

"Any tensions that there might have been, were soon dissipated. My colleagues from work met me and past attitudes were no more. They were all pleased to see me and welcomed me with open arms. I was now one of them. We were comrades in arms!

"They introduced me to other members at the meeting and inevitably told them the story of my altercation with the deputy on the pit-top. It became the topic of conversation and the facts changed and the incident became one of major consequence. It assumed an unwarranted importance in the minds of many of those at the meeting.

"I hardly ever spoke at these meetings. I would just sit there and listen. It was obvious that even amongst those on the floor that there were divisions and factions. There was a Communist group represented by Jackie Crane and the Labour Party by Bill Roome.

"It was plain to see that there was some dissatisfaction with the members on the platform. There was talk that they were 'Gaffers' Men' and were on the take. The chairman and secretary appeared most unsympathetic to those who questioned them. At times they appeared to treat any critical comments with ill-considered contempt. Little did they seem to realise that they would lose support by such actions. The chairman felt that he knew best, and he would make it quite plain that he did know best.

"I did not make my thoughts known on the floor of the meeting. I kept such notions as I had to myself. I did join in conversation with other men during the intervals. Sometimes we just passed the time of the day or talked of general politics, or about our families and what it was like to live in this part of Kent. We all got on well together and life was altogether more pleasant. Though the work underground was hard at 'snap time' we would chat and laugh and during work we would help each other.

"This is how life should be. I was content when I arrived back home after work. The wife would ask me how the day went and when I replied that the day went well, a big happy smile would come to her face. We knew we had a future!

"I attended several meetings during the latter half of 1917 and early in 1918, during which time the Annual General Meeting was held. It was at this meeting that the officers and committee were elected for the following year. I had listened to what the men had said and realised that feelings ran deep and that there was a wide feeling of dissatisfaction with the present representatives. Groups had got together to try to depose the present holders of office. I kept well out of it. I was a newcomer and felt it wise to keep my own counsel. Would anything happen? Would any one challenge the platform?

"The chairman declared the meeting open, and then vacated the chair. The secretary took over and proceeded with the first business which was to elect a chairman for the ensuing year. There was a sudden quiet in the hall, a moment of silence which was broken by a lone voice proposing the outgoing chairman be elected for another year. He was duly seconded. This procedure was followed for the election of secretary and members of the committee. There was a small change in the make-up of the committee when two new members were elected but it was obvious that the main power remained with the chairman and secretary.

"It did not give much hope that attitudes or policies would change. It did not augur well for the future. It was felt by a number of members, that the chairman and secretary were in the management's pocket, and they were not to be trusted to act in the best interests of the workmen.

"It was during a glorious summer's day in July 1918 that a bye-election took place to fill a vacancy on the committee. Much to my surprise my name was put forward. The chairman asked if I was willing to stand. There was a moments silence when the atmosphere seemed filled with a certain tenseness, mixed with expectancy and apprehension. You could feel the unsaid words, 'Go for it Billy! Go for it!' I made up my mind to accept the nomination and thus I was elected to the committee in July 1918. It had all happened so quickly, in less than a year, and all because of what seemed to me a minor incident on the pit-hill, that altercation between myself and a deputy."

Chapter 17

My election as Secretary of Tilmanstone Miners Union.
January 1919--1946.

"I talked matters over with my wife, Margaret, and said it was not in my nature to keep quiet if I felt strongly about something, I would have to join in discussions and make my views known. So it was some 6 months later, at the following Annual General Meeting in January 1919 that I was elected to the position of Secretary of Tilmanstone Miners Union, a position I held until September 1946, a period of some twenty-seven years.

"Those early years immediately after my election were troubled and full of unrest, within the local mining community and in the country generally. There was trouble even within the armed forces. Though the reasons for dissension were very different, word spread of what was happening and it deeply affected attitudes of the general public.

"There were the international events, including the continued fighting in Russia after the Revolution in 1917. Some members of the government, including Winston Churchill, supported sending armed forces to fight with the White Russians and depose the Soviets. Ernie Bevin and the Dockers Union refused to transport any troops to Russia. Political attitudes and actions were changing fast. There seemed a growing instability in the country and a hardening of attitudes in some quarters."

Chapter 18

Demands of Private Owners.
Attempts to Crush the Union. The Evans Case.

The war ended in November 1918, and not much time passed before the owners approached the government and demanded the return of their property. They demanded the mines be returned to private ownership. The civil unrest through-out the country threatened political stability. Lloyd George did not want such troubles extending to the miners.

Realising the strongly held opinions of the miners and the growing power of the Miners Unions, the government played for time, after all the miners made up a substantial part of the British workforce, some 10 per cent. It was felt that with the unrest which had occurred in other industries, and some parts of the armed forces, this was no time to foment further conflict and possible violence in another large section of the population.

It was thus that the government appointed a Royal Commission consisting of 3 mine owners, 3 industrialists and 3 economists including Sydney Webb and R.H. Tawney, under the chairmanship of Mr Justice Sankey. It came out with conflicting reports. The Majority Report favoured permanent nationalisation and the Minority Report an immediate return to private ownership.

The promise of the government that it would implement the recommendations of the Sankey Report was not carried out. The miners felt let down. A promise had been broken, their expectations were dashed. Playing to both sides Lloyd George proposed that the miners be guaranteed existing wage levels and a 7 hour working day but that the mines revert to private ownership.

Growing Unrest in the Mines. 1920s.

Locally amongst the working men there was growing anger. This was not a question of propositions made by the officials or the Union as an organisation, it arose from the grass roots, from the coal face workers themselves. Their claims were ignored. Their expectations were not being addressed. This unrest expressed itself in different ways, often in sectional and unofficial strikes. In some quarters there was talk of take-over of property by the miners, even if this involved force and violence. The weekly Union meetings were packed out.

In 1920 the Miners Federation demanded a wage increase with the threat of strike action if their demand was rejected. The government announced at the same time its plans to return the mines to private ownership. This of course was met with jubilation by the mine owners. The dockers and railwaymen were reticent about the form of action to be taken by the Miners Union. They did not rally to the support of the miners. This may have been as much due to personal differences between the leaders, the manner of their behaviour to one another as to any genuine principle. The owners seeing these divisions in the Union leadership adopted a more aggressive approach toward the workforce. Now was the time to act. The local management became more belligerent in their actions.

It was January 1919 that Billy Newman was elected secretary of the Tilmanstone Miners Union. His first act was to consult with the rest of the committee and find out whether there were any matters that the members considered urgent and should be acted upon.

The first item of concern, was the manner and form of approach to be adopted when dealing with local management. There was a great deal of anger among the workmen. Feelings ran deep. There was a demand for action, for action now!

Different opinions were expressed but it was agreed by the committee that as representatives of the men, it was incumbent that we do the best for the men. We needed at the end of the day to bring something out for the men, even if it was not what we had demanded. We should accept the best offer that we could get in the circumstances. This would entail a process of negotiations which assumed a degree of trust and good will on both sides. We would need to be united.

During those early days of 1919 and 1920, time after time we found ourselves up against a brick wall. The answer to any of our requests, however reasonable, was, "No! No! always No!".

The men had shown a great deal of restraint during those early months, but were now becoming restless, quarrelsome and some might even be provoked into violence. These men were honest workmen but they were tough men. They not only exhibited their strength in the nature of the work they undertook, they were tough mentally. They had shown their strength of moral fibre in undertaking such long journeys' with little means to establish new lives in a distant part of the country. These were men of strong will, and strength of character. They knew what they wanted.

The committee met to discuss what was becoming a serious situation. The officers of the committee reported to the meeting and stated bluntly that they could get nowhere through negotiation. The committee had all tried hard, they had done their best but the door of management was always closed. The only alternative was to fight. "This meant that we must be ready to back up any threats we might make with 'effective action'."

It would be necessary, to closely consider any suggested action and examine any possible consequences that might arise from such action. For the Union to count at all, it needed as much support as possible. It was vital that we build up the membership of the Union. The aim was 100 percent membership, a "Closed Shop" the objective.

This became our main policy for the next few weeks. All members of the committee and some men unofficially joined in the efforts to recruit members to the Union. It soon came to the notice of Billy that some enthusiasts, in their desire to recruit as many members as possible, were adopting more imaginative methods than were entirely legitimate .There was some talk in the pubs that those unwilling to join the Union should be sent to Coventry, others even talked in terms of "tar and feathering", mostly beer talk. When this came to the notice of Billy Newman, he let it be known that any such actions which openly or otherwise involved threats were to be stopped. This was made quite clear to all the men. Reason, persuasion, persistence and enthusiasm in a spirit of friendship, this was the best way forward. The object was to build a committed group of workmen who would be there to support their comrades in time of trouble as well as in the good times.

Within 3 months their efforts were proving demonstrably successful.

Attempts to Crush the Union and the Evans Case.
Sufficient numbers had joined to make Tilmanstone Miners Union an organisation of power and influence. The Union representatives now had greater strength when going into negotiations. The manager did not appear to realise that he now faced a new situation. To him everything remained the same. It appeared that his mission in life was to break the Union, and this he was determined to do. This he stated in conversations with my father. All approaches at negotiations were rejected. The Union representatives were getting no-where. The only course of action was to make it clear that they would fight and they would have the men solidly behind them.

Billy made one final approach to the manager, who after a short conversation made it quite clear there was no room for compromise. He ran the pit and no miner or Union member was going to tell him what to do and if it came to a contest the Union would suffer. The men would regret any action they might take against the management.

These findings were reported back to the committee so that the men knew exactly where they stood and were fully informed of what the consequences might be. They were to be in no doubt, that this was no place for the faint hearted.

The Evans case.

The manager, emboldened by the behaviour of the owners, and the comment in the press that the national leaders of the Unions were divided, felt that a pre-emptive strike would be a good tactic. He visited the pit one night and claimed that the 'Winder' Jack Evans was away from his control post and he sacked him, and Valentine his assistant, on the spot.

Mr Evans, a member of the Union committee, was well respected. The 'Assistant Winder' spoke up for Mr Evans. They had had been stretching their legs as was the custom and talking about what they might do at the end of the shift. The 'Assistant Winder' said it was most unusual for the manager to be on the premises particularly during the night shift. In fact, it was to the best of his knowledge, the first time this had occurred.

Mr Evans denied being that far away from his controls as to constitute any danger.

The Union stood by Mr Evans and requested that an "Independent Committee of Inquiry" be set up to consider the case, weigh up the evidence and make a judgement. The manager refused to consider the request and so a strike was called in support of the Union's claim.

It was made clear that the Union would abide by any decision emanating from such an inquiry. If it found against Mr Evans, then he would lose his job!

This was put to the management, but it was still determinedly turned down. The challenge appeared to be, "Do your worst! You will regret it!"

The Union balloted its' members and received overwhelming support that a strike be called in support of the "call for an Inquiry". The men had decided that the time had come to fight. As the strike continued, the fight grew in bitterness. Black-legs were brought in. Deputies were used to work the pumps. It proved difficult for the management to keep the mine working since they had to pump 2 million gallons of water every 24 hours.

The men were out for "three weeks and three days," standing loyally behind the leadership. The great wheels of Tilmanstone Colliery no longer turned. No coal came up the pit. The Union adopted the tactic of engaging the men while they were on strike to march in orderly lines round the pit to ensure no damage was done to any equipment, and to give the men some sense of purpose while unable to work.

The management did not trust the men to behave in a non-violent and disciplined way, so they employed the police to protect pit property. They had to pay the police for this protection, driving up their costs. The police were on continuous duty, at one time facing some two hundred miners patrolling in the pit yard.

One afternoon the superintendent of the police, Superintendent Stone, approached Billy and commented that the action was causing a lot of strife on both sides and wouldn't it be a good idea for the Union to call off the strike, since nobody appeared to be benefiting from the action?

The reply was "Can you blame us for wanting justice? We were asking for no more than an Independent Inquiry." Billy continued, "I feel sure that if you, superintendent, found yourself in a similar situation, you would have no hesitation in granting that such an inquiry be set up. All that we are asking for is fundamental British justice. And so we parted."

Mr Billy Newman managed to arrange a meeting in London with representatives of the board of directors to see whether they might reach some form of solution and agree to the Union's request. Some days later, Mr McCurrel was sent down from the Ministry of Labour. "We met him and in the course of discussions he proposed, 'that if the men immediately returned to work, an impartial tribunal would be held within fourteen days at which Mr Evans would be allowed to state his case; this, on condition that the Union would accept the decision of the tribunal whatever that might be.' This we felt was a successful conclusion. It is just what we had fought for. The strike was called off, and the men returned to work.

"Sometime later I was walking from the White Horse to the pit, when the manager drove past. Such was his hurry that a few hundred yards further on, he crashed through some railings. When I caught up I immediately, with others, helped lift the car back on the road. He, in his temper, turned on me and said, 'You are to blame for this Newman! You decided to stop the pit and I'm hurrying to keep it open. I've already been in touch with Mr McCurrel and he has instructed me to take certain actions.'

"He proceeded to the pit. I followed and went straight into the office and took a witness with me. I stayed and did not come out of the office until the last man had gone down the pit."

An Inquiry was held as promised. A Mr J. C. Roscamp, HM Inspector of Mines was in charge. After a thorough hearing the members of the Inquiry came down in favour of Evans. Mr Roscamp reported that "Evans did not leave his post in any neglectful way that might cause danger."

On receipt of this report, members of the Union committee met the Chairman of the Board of Directors, Professor Gallway and his associates, and within a short time they agreed to a full reinstatement of Evans and Valentine, both of whom started work the following day.

The company had to pay the full cost for the police protection. If the miners had caused a single incident and been responsible for any damage, the cost of police protection would have been charged to the council and paid through the Rates. The fact that no incident occurred speaks well for the discipline of the men and this gave their representatives great satisfaction. After six months the manager left the colliery and a new manager was appointed.

The men had been willing to make a sacrifice because they had come to trust the leadership. The men themselves had been fully consulted and were made to feel part of the decision. It was their decision. It was their fight and it was their victory.

This did not mean that the troubles with the management ceased. Far from it. The local management did not change the way they dealt with Union representatives. The management looked upon them as a nuisance and an inconvenience that they did their best to ignore. They did their best to refuse to give the Union any sign of official recognition.

Chapter 19

National Unrest a Major Public Concern.

The struggle between the colliery owners and the miners was on-going. It did not just apply to one locality, but extended across the country. It was a national struggle. The importance of this situation became a central concern of politics and extended into the realms of government.

General unrest in the country had become a major matter of public concern which politicians could no longer ignore. This involved people right across the industrial spectrum and even extended to professional organisations, and armed forces.

Quotes from G.D.H. Coles' writings in the 'Common People', page 534, published by Methuen, 1938.

"In August 1918 the 'London Police' came out on strike and met with some success. The situation in the Army appeared no better. 'Soldiers' Councils' were actually reported from Egypt, and insubordination and mutinies occurred at home. It was reported that 10,000 soldiers mutinied on January 6th at Folkestone, 2,000 at Dover and some 60,000 at various other camps across the Country.

"Intermittent riots continued well into the summer. Five

people were killed and 21 wounded in one riot at Kimmel Park, and Epsom Police Station was stormed and the station sergeant killed.

"These acts of violence looked like spreading and threatening civil life through-out the country.

"Strikes that occurred in the mines in Yorkshire and in the London Underground were to that date relatively peaceful. However, on the Clyde in Glasgow there occurred almost pitched battles between the workers and the police. E. Shinwell, David Kirkwood and Willie Gallacher stood their ground in the face of intense police batoning.

"Such strikes were on going and were becoming more frequent. The worst, it appeared, was still to come."

In the 1920s the miners at the grass roots were in a militant mood. They voted in favour of a national strike demanding an increase in wages. The Miners Union tried to persuade the other partners in the Triple Alliance to come out in support, but without success. The miners left alone, continued in their course of action and struck by themselves.

The strike only lasted a few weeks and terms were agreed "that there should be a wage increase dependent upon output." Though the miners had achieved part of their objective in gaining an increase in pay it was because of the promise made by the Cabinet, to implement the recommendations of the first "Sankey Report", that the miners called off their strike.

The big Unions had publicly displayed the weakness of their bargaining position when confronted by the government. They displayed a lack of unity, "in the action that should be taken." The conclusion drawn from the recent situation, might justifiably be that the idea of a general strike, was very much still an idea. It was still something of the imagination rather than a matter of possible reality. In the political mind it was unlikely to happen. The government and the owners were still dominant. The government took its' revenge by passing the "Emergency Powers Act", which gave the government extensive powers to deal with strikes in "essential industries".

Chapter 20

The Rich Culture and Talent of the Miners.

Though many of the intellectuals, including the Fabians were sympathetic to the miners and their cause, the words of Beatrice Webb as recorded in her diary reveal an underlying attitude of mind toward the working class by many of the intellectuals. She is recorded as writing, "The miners are among the best paid of manual workers they are earning, as a matter of fact, as much money as they can spend in their comparatively low state of civilisation."

"The low state of civilisation," being the operative words!

This to me demonstrates the great gap that existed between the different social classes. They were virtually closed communities and were often ignorant of the ways in which each group lived. This illustration of Beatrice Webb gives the impression that the main interest of the Webbs, and their group, was one of intellectual superiority and of "power and influence", rather than their willingness to investigate and make explicit what they mean by "their (the miners') low state of civilisation". The implication being that even if they had higher wages, they would not know how to put it to good use. This to me demonstrates an uncalled for intellectual arrogance on the part of some of the more fortunate and influential members of society.

The rich culture of many of the mining communities is well illustrated by the many Miners' Male Voice Choirs, particularly in the Valleys of South Wales and in the North. In Yorkshire and Durham the miners were well known with their famous brass bands. The non-conformist religious groups were strong. The chapels were full and in various parts of the country the Salvation Army was growing in strength.

In some areas, the Miners Union became the hub of civic affairs. Workmens institutes were established which included libraries and facilities for community activities and in some areas even hospitals were built, founded and funded by the miners. Maesteg, in the valleys of South Wales is an example of such action.

The Workers Education Association was attracting great interest and support in the mining communities attracting a wealth of rich talent. There was intense discussion not only of local problems but of those extending abroad to include the real and serious concerns of international affairs. They were adept at expressing ideas and many, such as Jim Griffiths, Ernie Bevin and latterly Aneurin Bevan established themselves as eminent public speakers. The craft unions and trades unions became a focus for many such activities, and proved rich in the expression of their diverse interests.

Intellect and talent were not the sole prerogative of the Webbs or the Fabians or the wealthy in society.

Chapter 21

The Fiasco caused by the National Miners Leaders in 1921. The prelude to the General Strike of 1926.

The coal mines, which had been taken into national ownership at the beginning of war, were still in public ownership. Now the war was over, the mine owners wanted their property back. In February 1919, some three months after Armistice Day, the mine owners demanded back that which they thought was rightfully theirs. They wanted the return of their collieries. They wished to operate them once more, so they could take the profits and make money.

The miners, the underground workers were very much against such a move. They made up a large proportion of the country's workforce, some 10 per cent. Lloyd George, the Prime Minister, did not wish to antagonise such a large section of the public, but he was being pressured by the very powerful group of wealthy mine owners. He sought a way out of this difficult situation, so he played for time.

As previously recorded, Lloyd George appointed the Sankey Commission to make a report.

Lloyd George did not carry out the Cabinet promise to implement Lord Sankey's recommendation, but tried to work out a deal to please both sides. For the miners he proposed that existing wage levels be guaranteed and a 7 hour working day be the norm. For the mine owners a return of their property. Plans to privatise the mines would be drawn up.

The Cabinet had previously promised that it would implement the recommendations of the Sankey Report which advocated continued nationalisation of the mines, but the government went back on its promise.

The miners felt let down and were very angry. They had returned to work after the strike of the 1920's, on the understanding that the government would fulfil its' promise. The result was a great deal of unrest in the mining industry, not only in Union offices, but more so, amongst the miners at the coal face. They were very angry! Feelings ran deep! They felt betrayed.

In the meantime the government had taken the opportunity to pass an "Emergency Powers Act", which gave them wide powers to deal with strikes in emergency services. This boded ill for the future of any actions that might be taken by the rade unions.

The mine workers feeling that the politicians had deserted them and had gone back on all their promises, at once demanded a wage increase, with the threat of strike action if their demands were not met.

The owners rejected the miners' demands out of hand and emboldened by what they saw as their chance of victory, demanded a new wage agreement involving a cut in wages. The miners refused the terms and the owners, who believed they were now in a dominant position, declared a "Lock Out".

The miners were refused employment unless they accepted the new conditions of payment as proposed by the owners, which included a reduction in wages.

Billy Newman, Tilmanstone Union Secretaty,
talking to Sir Thomas Poulson, MP.

On April 1, 1921, a million miners refused to accept the terms laid down by the owners and were declared unemployed. They refused to work under the terms of the new contract. Many of the mines closed. The pit villages were silent. This was not a strike originally declared by the miners. It was a "Lock-out", declared by the owners.

The Union, faced with pit closures, was forced into a ballot of members to see whether they were prepared to accept the proposed contract or make the stoppage of work official by calling for strike action. Such action was legally necessary for the Union to be able to support its' members.

Chapter 22

Miners Strike of 1921 And the Fiasco brought about by Actions of the Miners Leaders.

The Trade and General Workers Union and The National Union of Railwaymen agreed in principle to support the miners, but there was dissension in the leadership. The miners' committee would not allow the leaders of the other unions to come into their meeting which discussed strategies and tactics that might involve them. They, including Ernie Bevin, were left standing outside, not knowing what was being discussed or decided. There was no real consultation or co-ordination with the other unions.

The miners decided to reject the new contract and not to seek mediation. The Unions agreed to recommend that their members be called upon to strike as from the 15th of April 1921.

However on the eve of the proposed strike, Frank Hodges, the General Secretary of the Miners Union, at a meeting of the National Council of Labour, told journalists that he was prepared to negotiate on behalf of the miners, new wage rates, area by area. The Prime Minister Mr Lloyd George immediately responded and invited Frank Hodges to a meeting where they might discuss terms and formalise some arrangements for further meetings.

Hodges had acted purely on his own initiative without consulting or informing any of his colleagues. It was a surprise to all, particularly among the local pitmen, where rumour and misinformation was rife.

The national executives of the unions, especially the miners were taken aback. They were completely shocked. The miners were absolutely dumbfounded when they first read of these comments in the morning newspapers.

The mine workers themselves, the dockers and railwaymen were bewildered. What the hell was happening? Was there a strike or not? What were they to do? There was puzzlement and anger amongst the men.

Neighbours gathered together, so shocked were they at what was happening. Men gathered in the club and at the pub. They gathered together wherever they might get the latest news, anxiously waiting for the latest announcement, remembering that there was no television, and few radios. Communications were very limited.

During the course of the day information came through that an emergency meeting of the Miners' Executive had been called to discuss the situation. The proposal of the General Secretary, Mr Frank Hodges, was turned down in the executive meeting by a majority of one and Frank Hodges resigned his position as General Secretary of the Miners Union. The miners went on strike without the support of the Transport and General Workers' Union or the railwaymen. The miners' leadership appeared to be in disarray. The miners were on their own.

After 10 weeks a ballot was held which produced a majority of 2 to 1 to continue the strike. The anger was still there. The sense of solidarity had increased in strength. There was a deep feeling of commitment and conviction that their cause was just and they were determined to fight for it. It took some 3 months for the men to be starved back to work. That day became embedded in the minds of the miners and was known as "Black Friday". This was in the year 1921, only three years after the end of the 1914-18 war.

National Confrontation. Govt. Owners acting together.
As it affected Tilmanstone.
This had been an all-out fight between the owners of the pits and the workers. The local management were now in their element. Their attitude had been directed by the owners who felt that with the implicit aid of the government, they could crush the unions.

Billy Newman had informed his committee and all the men of the latest developments. The men were solid in their support of Union policy in 1921.

"No to Reduction in Wages."
"No to an increase in Hours."

The only men allowed to work were the safety men and the men on the pumps to prevent flooding. None of the workmen would accept the terms offered by the management. There were to be no negotiations. The men were initially "locked out", now they were on strike and the pit wheels were stilled! The mine was silent. There was no coal being mined.

The owners, the government, the national press and the B.B.C. were used to undermine the position of the Union. False information was sent out to give the impression that the strike was weakening and that in some areas men were going back to work. The Daily Herald was banned by the government so the miners produced their own broadsheet. The Tilmanstone Union organised soup kitchens and gave direct help to those in urgent need.

It was important to discuss any problems of concern with all the men at full and open union meetings. It was important that the men feel that the decisions made were their decisions, that they were in charge.

There was always a danger that by staying at home, deprived of that routine and purpose that work gives, some men might fall into a state of "complacency". Activity, and purpose were essential to the maintenance of good morale. At Tilmanstone, as in the 1920's, for those willing to take part, the men were organised in shifts to march round the pit to ensure the safety of pit property, and prevent any possibility of vandalism. Such tactics also meant that the management would have to employ the police since they distrusted the miners being on the edge of the pit top. This involved payment of the police by the owners, thus increasing their costs. The manager, it is reputed, hired cars to drive round the pit with full headlights shining on the men and recording names. It was an obvious attempt to intimidate the men, but without success.

Billy was called out to attend to several minor incidents; incidents which even scared the daylights out of those involved.

On one occasion, a miner having had a little more beer than was good for him, approached the pit top and was threatening to throw an explosive grenade down the shaft. The only person he would talk to was Billy Newman. When he arrived Billy diffused the situation and after a short time persuaded the man to part with the grenade. He escorted him home, but just before they got there. the man turned and with a big smile on his face, said "You know Billy there's plenty more where that came from. Anyway, I never intended to throw it down the shaft. I just wanted to see what you would do. But it did put the fear of god into those fellas. You know Billy they are boss's men."

The Return to Work.
At last the Miners' Executive felt that the workers had been out long enough. They and their families had endured a great deal of suffering. It was decided that no good purpose would be served by prolonging the strike. The government were adamant in refusing the miners demands. The Miners National Executive felt that there was no more the miners could do and therefore recommended that the men return to work. This recommendation was put before a full meeting of Tilmanstone mineworkers at which it was decided to accept the Executives' decision "that the men return to work".

After so much sacrifice this was a sad, sad day for the men. They had so much hoped for a successful outcome and they were a proud group of men. These men felt, they knew they had right on their side and that their friends and families were being sacrificed, for the sake of the profits of already rich men.

The miners now had to accept the terms laid down by the owners which were that wages would be negotiated area by area and that some pits would have to take cuts, and pay wages below subsistence level.

The miners blamed their defeat on the leadership of the other unions who refused to give them their full support and call their members out on strike.

Chapter 23

The Local Union Initiatives at Tilmanstone Colliery

The main initial concern of the local committee not only at Tilmanstone but at the other Kent pits was to ensure that the men continued to stick together and remain members of the Union.

Billy Newman besides being secretary of the committee at Tilmanstone Colliery with the full confidence of the members of the Union was elected to the office of President of the Kent Mineworkers Association in 1921, which included Tilmanstone, Snowdown, Chislet and Bettshanger. He held this position for 12 years until 1933.

Billy Newman chairing the Committee of the Kent Mineworkers Association, 1921.

The worst time during these years, when he became known for his aggression and militancy, had been between 1919 culminating in the 1921 national strike. During that time, backed by a talented and enthusiastic committee, they had built up a quite fearsome reputation. The Union at Tilmanstone had now become a reliable and effective force. They had managed to maintain the membership in spite of the heart-breaking defeat they had to endure in 1921. The men were well disciplined and knew what was expected of them.

During the latter period of the twenties, any local miners problems that occurred, and there were many, were resolved by hard bargaining.

Sometime later, referring to his character and general leadership during his many years as secretary, Mr David Jenkins who was clerk and chief finance officer to the management of Tilmanstone Colliery, writing about Billy Newman said, "He was instrumental as Secretary of the Union in successfully negotiating the first wages agreement for the workmen of Tilmanstone Colliery and afterwards the first district wages agreement for the combined Kent coalfield."

He continues, "It speaks well of his leadership that while instrumental in getting for the workers of Tilmanstone Colliery the highest wages paid in the Kent coalfield and thereby achieving the highest output per man shift, only one days' local stoppage occurred through strikes from 1921 to 1946"

Chapter 24

Events that changed the National and Social Landscape.

These were momentous times. There had been the Great War during which time, the nature of war had completely changed. No longer did it consist of comparatively small professional armies operating in some far distant country, now they were massed armies, and the effects of war were felt close to home. It touched every family in the land. In this country the small regular army had to be supported with greatly increased numbers. Volunteers were called for and a great patriotic fervour swept the country.

A whole generation of young men joined the Army prepared to go to war and fight for their 'King and Country'. They were working men from the mines, from industry and from the farms. There were the rich young men from the landed gentry. They came from all sections of society. The working men provided the foot-soldiers. The wealthy were put in charge, made officers of the regiments and they all marched off to war.

Though there was still this marked division of men from the different social classes, the very nature of warfare, the dependence for their very existence, one with another, lead to changing attitudes. Class divisions began to soften. The objectives and claims on the part of working men for a better life were being recognised by a growing number of the middle classes as 'just claims'. Political groupings which had been established before 1914 started to become active once again and attracted large numbers from across the broad social spectrum. They became vocal in their support for a more caring society.

A Land Fit for Heroes.

As the war drew to its' close, the cry was for a 'land fit for heroes'. On demobilisation, the soldiers, all wanted good conditions when they returned home. Many of the officers who had lived in the trenches with these men and had fought side by side with them, and often owed their lives to their comrades across the social divide, supported their cause. The working men coming home from the war wanted jobs, they wanted money to provide for their families. They felt that this was the least they should have. They voiced their opinions in public, organised public demonstrations and joined in political meetings.

The two main parties represented in Parliament at this time were the Tory party and the Liberal party. Other groups outside Parliament were increasing in influence. They were mostly left wing parties, off-shoots of the more militant trade unions. These included the Social Democratic Federation, the Independent Labour Party, the Fabian Society and some candidates such as Victor Grayson who fought as independents on a purely socialist programme.

The very manner in which the government intervened in private industrial disputes forced the unions to become more politicised. It was not until February 1900 that the Labour Representation Committee was formed which was colloquially called "The Labour Party". It was an attempt to bring the left wing movements together under one umbrella, forming one organisation that would represent the working man.

J. Ramsay MacDonald was elected secretary and started recruiting trade union branches to support the setting up of independent Labour members as parliamentary candidates. His efforts met with rapid success though some people on the right of the party would not join the new organisation because they thought it had gone far too much to the left, while the Social Democratic Federation denounced it, as "in no way being socialist" and as such, it would be an obstacle to the establishment of a socialist society. These criticisms were largely ignored by the unions and the new organisation flourished.

Many local unions became interested and saw this organisation as a way to achieve their ends.

The trade unions had from the first been organised on an industrial and trade basis. Private ownership, both of property and the means of production, was recognised as the method of economic organisation. The owners sought to organise production in their industries, their factories and in the mines at the lowest possible costs. If this meant low wages and poor conditions at work, then this was a state of affairs the workforce would have to face. Individual workers were looked upon and treated solely as a means of production. All that mattered in this system was the important question of supply. A sufficient wage would be paid that would ensure a sufficient supply of labour. This entailed production for maximum profit, which in turn meant production at lowest cost. Initially the workforce joined together in unions to give them sufficient strength when facing the owners in an endeavour to protect their pay and conditions at work. Rarely were the living conditions of the workforce regarded by the owners, as any part of their responsibility. The workforce had to make claims for better conditions and it had to fight for them.

The Union representatives had seen their role primarily as industrial, taking their concerns directly to the management and the owners of the industry. Though some individuals such as Keir Hardy became Members of Parliament with the help of the Liberal Party, initially the unions did not follow the parliamentary route to achieve their ends.

It was rather the owners, well represented in government, who employed the weapons of the state, relying on the government to pass laws that restricted the freedoms of the unions to act. It was thus that the unions, to strengthen their position, found it necessary to enter the political realm. Most of the early unions were local unions, representing the local workforce. In the course of time many joined together on a regional basis such as the Durham Miners. It was sometime later that the National Union of Mineworkers became the dominant organisation.

The urgent need was that the grassroots form strong local organisations.

Billy Newman was building up strong support among the miners and their families, by working for them in his capacity as Secretary of Tilmanstone Miners Union. He made contacts in the course of his official work with doctors and solicitors who often gave him free advice. As a result he was often able to help people with their personal problems as well as those relating to Union matters.

His reputation spread through-out the local countryside, beyond the mining community, embracing the farmers and local agricultural workers. He would often cycle 4 or 5 miles to outlying villages to visit people who asked for his help. He never asked what their political affiliation might be. If anybody needed help he would give it.

Billy was one of those who felt that the Union should become involved in politics in every sense of that word. He was very well aware of the struggles that were taking place both in this country and on the continent. He was deeply conscious of the political issues that confronted the working class. He was widely read, acquainted with the writings of Marx and Engels, and of the French Socialist Jean Jaure, tragically assassinated at the beginning of the First World War. Well-thumbed copies of 'Das Capital', Webb's 'History of Trade Unionism', and Tawney's brilliant writings in his 'Acquisitive Society', adorned his bookshelf. He was well acquainted with many people active in politics.

A group of socialists had formed the Independent Labour Party which broke away from the Liberals as early as 1893 in an attempt to form a working class party. However according to Lord Shepherd, a former National Agent, it was not until 1909 that the Miners' Federation of Great Britain entered into affiliation with the then Labour Party. Prior to this action trades unions had sought to work through the good offices of members of the Liberal Party.

During the eighteen eighties two socialist societies came into existence. They were the Social Democratic Federation with the full doctrine of Karl Marx, and the Fabian Society providing programmes for the trades unions which the more moderate supporters were pleased to accept. The Fabian Society wielded influence far beyond what might be expected of such an organisation. It owed much to the dedication and ingenuity of its founder members Beatrice and Sydney Webb, George Bernard Shaw, Graham Wallas, Sydney Olivier, R.B. Haldane of the University of London, and Kingsley Martin, many of whom managed to gain the ear of those in authority.

One of their fundamental principles, as expounded by Beatrice Webb in her diary 1903, was that, "Our general social policy is to construct a base to society in the form of a legally enforced 'minimum standard of life', and to develop all forms of shooting upwards... whether of individuals or of discoveries and refinements." Among their lasting accomplishments were the establishment of the London School of Economics and the weekly publication 'The New Statesman'.

In 1893 the Independent Labour Party pledged to socialist principles, attracted much attention and support with its claim to work toward the creation of a working-class party. The I.L.P. soon captured the imagination of the more active spirits in the trade union movement.

At the 1899 Trade Union Congress, a resolution was passed which instructed "the Parliamentary Committee to invite the cooperation of the cooperative, socialistic, trade union and other working class organisations - to devise ways and means for securing the return of an increased number of Labour members to the next Parliament."

Richard Bell and Keir Hardie were not the only working class representatives sent to the 1900 Parliament. There were nine other working class members elected through the hard work of individual trades unions.

The 1906 Election was a victory for the Labour Party. It had now become an established party, a force to be taken seriously. Out of fifty candidates standing, twenty nine were elected. On the green benches in the House of Commons they looked like a real party compared with the four lone figures of the previous Parliament.

The Osborne Judgement. Labour a Challenge to Authority.
The ruling class and big business saw this situation as a challenge to their authority. The rising power of the Labour Party had to be stopped. The government action took the form of an attack on the unions' ability to raise money to support Labour candidates. This they accomplished by arranging that a railway employee seek an injunction to restrain the Union from levying its members to support the Labour Party. The injunction was upheld and any such monies spent by unions for political purposes would in future be illegal. This was known as the Osborne Judgement and it was not until 1913 that the Osborne Judgement was reversed by an act of Parliament giving the unions greater freedom to act politically. It could once more use union funds to spend on political party issues.

The real breakthrough for the working people, however, came in 1918, at the end of the war, when Parliament extended the franchise. Men over 21 with certain qualifications and women over the age of 30 were given right to vote.

Most of the young men who had gone off to fight for their King and Country and died on the battlefields of the Somme, at Ypres and at Passchendaele had never had the right to vote. They had played no part in the decision to make war. It was the rich and powerful who had decided their fate. The rulers, the rich and the powerful in Great Britain, Austria, Germany, France and Russia, were the people who decided whether there was to be war or peace.

In 1918 the numbers on the electoral roll in this country, increased over threefold and numbered some 21,370,316 and as Beatrice Webb notes in her diaries, "the coming of the Labour Party as a political force has been largely occasioned by this year's extension of the franchise." June 16th 1918.

Chapter 25

Local Parties.
The Formation of the Dover Labour Party 1920

At this time the organisation and decision making within the Labour Party was in the hands of a few influential people and controlled from the centre. The groups in charge were made up mostly of those representing national organisations, trades union bosses, and elite activists from the universities who joined such organisations as the Fabians, and the Social Democratic Party. There were few established local parties at this time though a number of candidates stood on an individual basis and gained some local support. It was however a rare case for such a candidate to stand a chance of being elected without being supported by a major organisation. The lone exception was the young Victor Grayson at the bye-election in Colne Valley in 1908.

It was about this time that local groups of working class people began to express their views and seek to participate in the organisation of the party, to which they felt they belonged. At the end of the Great War people joined in demonstrations. They were moved to action now they had the right to vote. It was in this situation that official constituency parties began to be established, and so in Dover May 1919 we see the beginnings of the formation of the Dover Labour Party, as it exists today in 1960.

Such was recorded in a local labour party journal by Mrs Florence Goodfellow. She writes.

"It was a bitterly cold spring evening in May 1919 when 13 people gathered round the stove in the grubby hall over the Cooperative Stores. It was a momentous little meeting for we were all ardent socialists met together to form "The Dover Local Labour Party". Arthur Goodfellow was elected the first chairman and Jimmy Goulden the secretary. The chairman and secretary and other members set to work to form a Divisional Party and one was soon started under the chairmanship of Billy Newman. Within a short space of time under his chairmanship there had been organised ten local parties and seven women's sections."

The efforts of all concerned were bearing fruit. The Dover Labour Party was on the move.

William Newman, first chairman of the Dover Divisional Labour Party in 1919, held that position for some ten years. The main political objective of the K.M.W.A. (Kent Mineworkers Association) was clearly defined when in 1921 it included in its' new rules the aim of securing "the complete abolition of private capitalism".

The combination of the two offices, the one as secretary of the Tilmanstone Miners Union and the other as chairman of the Dover Divisional Labour Party, gave force to Billy's power and status. They provided a base for him to extend his influence and open doors whereby he might get to know people and gain information and help when needed. He was very much an activist. He believed in going out and meeting people as well as doing office work. He still earned his living as a working miner below ground.

Carrying out the functions of such positions entailed a great deal of time and effort. During this time he was living at 14 Glenfield Road, Dover. This was his family home, the place where he lived during those crucial years from 1917 to 1927. As secretary of the Union, the years from 1919 to 1925 were the most difficult years. The managers of the pit adopted a very aggressive attitude and were rarely willing to negotiate or listen with any degree of understanding to any concerns the men might have. He was fortunate to have the full support of his fellow committee members who stood by him during some difficult times. By his actions Billy gained respect and made some powerful friends.

The early days of the Labour Party were both eventful and exciting. He was meeting many people of similar conviction who were keen to help and who became dedicated to the cause. They would meet in their spare time and go door-knocking, talking to people, trying to evoke interest in the cause of the Labour Party. It was fertile ground, for this was something new to the district and in response to the enthusiasm of the active workers, a great deal of support was found. This initial success was most encouraging.

Billy was brought up in the hard school of politics. Like so many others, he started from nothing. He had nothing except his own beliefs, a dedication and determination and a willingness to give of his time. It was a time of the hard politics of the street, provoking fierce debate and argument. It was a tough school of learning. All who took part had to ignore cheap ridicule and put up with hard insults. This was the nature of street politics conducted in largely tough working class areas.

At one such meeting organised on Deal seafront, a rather hostile group gathered and threatened to throw Billy and his friends into the sea. Needless to say, since the Police were present, the threats came to nothing, but the meeting closed early!

Syd Dye, Agent. And the Nature of Street politics.

At these open air meetings numbers of those attending demonstrated their interest by offering to support the party and a number even applied to become paid up members. The committee members were pleased with the progress being made, in establishing the party as a going concern, and as Mrs Goodfellow reports in her article, branches of the party were soon to be found in a number of villages across the constituency

Members of the committee congratulated those who had taken part in recruiting new members to the cause, and were quite enthusiastic that the actions and methods pursued should carry on. Some volunteered to help. The times and places of meetings were announced.

Sunday morning arrived, a fine sunny morning and it was time for the meeting to begin. A small group of curious onlookers had gathered, but where were those members who had shown such enthusiasm at the committee meeting? Had they all slept late?

The most loyal and effective supporter that Billy spoke of was his friend Sydney Dye, who acted as agent. The two of them would meet together at regular times and at set places on a Sunday morning with their soap-box. They would take turns who was to be the speaker and who the heckler. It was seeing these two fiercely arguing with one another that would attract the curious and the interested. Small crowds gathered to see what was happening. Some asked questions and joined in the discussion. Some were openly hostile and expressed themselves sometimes in violent terms. Both speakers, Billy and Syd, had a good sense of humour and a capacity for laughter which attracted many of the doubters and appealed to many in the crowd. At the end of the meeting, a few often showed a positive interest and would ask when they would be meeting again. Some even asked if they could join the Party, and they soon, gradually, built up the membership.

Sydney Dye was part of a farming family in Norfolk where he returned and made his home. A lifelong member of the Labour Party, he gained a seat in Parliament in the 1945 election and became a close friend of Hugh Gaitskell. He was a dedicated worker both in Parliament and in his constituency and held his seat with increased majorities at subsequent elections. He often came down from London to visit the family at Eythorne. Sadly however, he was killed in a car accident whilst driving to his home in Norfolk after attending the House of Commons in London.

Labour agent Syd Dye organising a day out for the Labour and Co-op women's group. Syd is in the rear, mother below him.

Visit of Shinwell and George Lansbury.

During those early days in Dover, mother entertained a number of Labour leaders. One such person was Emanual Shinwell who stayed with the family before going to open the pit head baths at Chislet Colliery.

As early as the 1930's the Labour Party had attracted sufficient support across the country-side, near Dover and Deal, but the core of support came from the mining community. It was a growing force in local politics.

During this time, Billy as Union Secretary and with the generous support of Tilden Smith, (the owner of the colliery), invited leading Labour figures such as George Lansbury, then leader of the Labour Party to address gatherings of miners and their families at fetes organised in the Mansion grounds at Eythorne.

Bennett, Labour Candidate. Astor wins.

The Labour Party had by now established itself in the Dover district as a recognisable force creating sufficient confidence among its members to put up a Labour candidate in the Parliamentary election. The year was 1935. The constituency funds were so low that an enthusiastic member offered to mortgage his house to ensure there was sufficient money to pay for the deposit. A Mr Bennett, Chairman of the local branch, was chosen as the Labour candidate and his opponent was the Conservative Major J. J. Astor. The road above Tower Hamlets called Astor Avenue is one of the places in Dover named after him.

Billy Newman's youngest son then about 7 years old attending Elvington Elementary School, still remembers the occasion well. "Major Astor visited the school one sunny afternoon and we were provided with cream cakes and tea. Whether this had anything to do with the election I don't know, but I do know that when I arrived home after school, on hearing my parents discussing the election, I told them they must vote for Mr Astor since he had given us some nice cakes! Dad just smiled." Mr Bennett got a substantial vote but failed to beat the popular Major J. J. Astor, who was once more returned as the Member of Parliament for Dover.

He served as Member of Parliament for Dover some 23 years. 1922-1945.

Chapter 26

Billy Newman elected to the Kent County Council.

The First Labour Kent County Councillor.

There was yet some success to be celebrated a few years later, when in 1939 the Labour Party contested the County Council seat for Eastry South. The area includes the mining communities of Elvington, and Aylesham, and the rural areas of St. Margarets and Eastry.

Billy Newman stood as the Labour candidate against Mr Rose of Sandwich, the Conservative. It had always been a Conservative seat, previously held by Lord Northbourne, who had been elevated to the Aldermanic Bench. The contest was fought with vigour, with vans going round decked with posters and loud speakers blaring:

"Vote! Vote! For Billy Newman!"

Support for Billy came from unexpected quarters, one being the owner of the cinema in Aylesham, an outward going, enthusiastic Mr Chipper. He gave his unreserved support including the use of his car.

The people of both Elvington and Aylesham composed largely of miners at Tilmanstone and Snowdown Pits, were most enthusiastic in their support. Meetings were held in the country villages of Eastry and Ash, as well as other outlying villages, and the support Billy received at them was surprising. The election was fought keenly by both parties, with no holds barred. Both parties were determined in their desire to win, though it was generally felt that the conservatives, with the much respected candidate in Mr Rose, from Sandwich, had the edge and would most likely take the day.

There was a record turnout creating an atmosphere of great excitement and not a little tension. Expectations on both sides were great. Though the Labour Party had the solid support of the mining community they were still a minority of the electorate and it was to the surprise of many that Billy

Newman was declared the winning candidate with a substantial majority. He became the first person and a working miner, to be elected as a Labour Member to the Kent County Council; the date, Monday, May 15th,1939. There were one or two Independents on the Kent County Council, including the very eloquent Rev Morgan of north Kent. The remaining Councillors were a solid group of Conservatives under the chairmanship of Sir Edward Hardie.

War broke out that same year, some four months after the election, on September 4th 1939, at 11.30 Sunday morning, when Prime Minister, Chamberlain announced to the nation, that we were at war with Germany. All further elections were suspended until the end of the war with Germany in 1945.

Chapter 27

Tilden Smith takes over Tilmanstone Colliery.
1925--1930.

The period from 1925 to 1930 was a particularly eventful time for Billy Newman as Secretary of the Tilmanstone Miners

Union. He was faced with four major events which were to have a great influence on the rest of his life.

The first was the take-over of the colliery by a new owner, Mr Tilden Smith, and the question was how to approach the management in this changed situation.

The second major issue that confronted the men was the prospect of being called out on a general strike in 1926, only one year after Mr Tilden Smith had become the new owner of Tilmanstone Colliery.

The third was the appointment of Dr. George Bell as Dean of Canterbury. The forth was the establishment of the Settlement at Elvington and making the acquaintance of some striking personalities including Brigadier Sir Wyndham Deedes, and Sir Ambrose Woodall of Manor House Hospital. Each of these events and the personalities involved were deeply to affect the life and outlook of Billy Newman.

The Coming of Tilden Smith.
In 1925, six years after Arthur Burr's death, Tilden Smith took control of Tilmanstone Colliery. Tilden became the new owner in 1925, a year in which labour relations at Tilmanstone were at an all-time low.

Nationally, across the country, feelings were running high, and unrest verging on violence was manifest in some parts of the mining industry. In that short period, since the end of the war, there had not been a time of settled industrial peace in the coal-fields. During 1920 and 1921, the frustration caused by the duplicity of the government and owners and the mixed messages of the miners' national leaders fostered a growing militancy among the mass of working miners. There developed a strong feeling for action. Talk was no longer enough, and so to preparations for the General Strike of 1926. As Mr Sherren, a relative of Tilden Smith writes, "Miners at Tilmanstone were notorious for their militant attitude". It was in this situation that Tilden Smith took charge.

It was in 1921 that Billy Newman, already Union Secretary at Tilmanstone, was elected President of the Kent Mineworkers Association. His was a growing influence. The manner in which he had been received by the previous management made him, to say the least, apprehensive about the new owner. Who was this man? What was he like? Trust and respect has to be earned!

In his previous dealings with the management of the mining industry and government, facts and actions were the only things Billy felt were to be trusted, not people. It was, "What was in the hand!" not, "What was on offer?" that counted. It was on this basis that Billy met Tilden for the first time.

The expectations remained very much as they had been during the earlier years of conflict. Everything would have to be fought for, after all Mr Tilden Smith had been engaged in dealings with Arthur Burr and those who had controlled Tilmanstone Colliery during the hard times in the post war period, including the 1920's. He was no small time investor but represented everything in the capitalist world that my father distrusted. He was a Director of the Burma Corporation, Channel Collieries Trust and Copper Mine Collieries as well as Burma Mines. His banking involvements, particularly as principal shareholder of the Share Guarantee Trust Ltd, had much bearing on most of the large projects undertaken by the various Kent companies.

When Tilden Smith bought Tilmanstone Colliery in 1925, he was in sole charge. He and his board of directors operated from his headquarters at Adelaide House, in London. He later acquired a mansion in lower Eythorne, in grounds which were situated about 800 yards from the pit. This made it possible for him to keep a close eye on the day to day activities of the workings at the pit and to acquaint himself with the details of the surrounding countryside. It put him in a position where he could better get to know the local people including the people of influence who had interests in the area, and from here he could closely study the area in terms of future developments.

From the start Mr Tilden Smith took a strong line and made it quite clear to the trade union and the men at the pit that he was in charge. Mr Sherren writes in his book that Tilden wanted to work with the men and that besides productivity he was concerned with the men's welfare. Tilden saw the men's welfare as an integral part of the economic process if you were aiming to achieve optimum productivity. However, he was a shrewd operator and a good judge of character, a wise and efficient pragmatist who could be quite ruthless, as witnessed by my father when Tilden removed a certain manager for impropriety.

When he first took over he was faced with union representatives, who were looked upon as hard liners, militant in their attitude and possible trouble-makers. Prior to Tilden's take over feelings of hostility had often ended in walk outs, with strikes and threats of unruly behaviour. This militancy was not exclusive to the miners of Tilmanstone. The miners of Chislet Colliery, at the village of Hersden, walked out in a series of strikes during 1921, again in 1922 and 1923. These were all disputes of a local nature, but a background to all this action was an expression of dissatisfaction felt by miners right across the country.

The owners began to flex their muscles. The headlines were that the miners would have to take a reduction in wages. Prime Minister Baldwin felt this was not the right time for the government to take any action that might be deemed provocative when there was so much unrest through-out the country. The Cabinet decided that of the choice "between a national strike and seeking an agreement with the Union," the latter was the best option. The government decided that the miners wages would be protected for nine months by a government subsidy which would cost some £10 million. In fact it cost twice as much, but the government thought they had bought peace at a bargain price. It was calculated that a strike would have cost £70 million. The unions declared a victory and called the 3 July 1925 "Red Friday".

Tilden Smith meets the Union Leaders.
There still remained the prospect of a general strike. The situation at this time contained all the ingredients of a toxic

mix which might explode at any moment into action of a most militant kind. Something needed to be done in an attempt to diffuse the situation. Locally, at Tilmanstone Colliery, Tilden Smith tried to do this by attempting to get the Union leaders in talks with him personally.

The Union leaders had decided, under the previous management, that they would at no time talk to the members of the management individually. They would only meet together as members of a team, and on official business.

Tilden Smith wanted to find the individual views of the union representatives and sound them out personally to see whether he might find some common ground on which they might get together in discussion and diffuse the troubled situation that existed. It is dangerous to assert specific motives to a particular ploy. One can give different opinions for the reasons a person acts in a such a manner. All I do know is the fact of my mother's first visit to the mansion.

I well remember my mother telling me of her first meeting with Mr Tilden Smith. He had requested that her husband, Billy Newman, the union secretary, meet him personally on a one to one basis to talk over any concerns he might have in dealing with the management. Billy refused and stated his position. He would only meet with Tilden Smith if he were accompanied by other members of the committee representing an official delegation, and that the business be recorded as official business.

Sometime later a chauffeur driven car, a Rolls Royce, arrived in the street outside no. 14 Glenfield Road, much to the surprise of the neighbours. It seemed so out of place. Their curiosity aroused they all came out to have a look. The chauffeur, dressed in his uniform, asked if this was where Mrs Newman lived. He knocked on the door and handed mother a message, which stated, "that her husband would collect her from Mr Tilden Smith's house after he had finished work. Would she please go and wait for him there!" Mother went and quickly got changed. She wondered what it was all about, but she was sufficiently convinced by the manner of the chauffeur and this impressive car that the message was genuine and so departed for Eythorne.

She was welcomed at Mr Tildens Smith's mansion, treated most courteously and made to feel completely at ease. Tilden had left a message at the pit, telling Billy that his wife was waiting for him at the mansion and would he come and collect her immediately after work.

This was to be the first time my father made personal contact on an individual basis with Mr Tilden Smith.

Mr Tilden Smith apologised for his subterfuge, but thanked Billy for coming. He felt it was the only way that they might get together and talk in a civilised manner. He had no wish to indulge in secret talks or make one sided bargains: all he wanted to do was to have a general conversation and that they should meet each other in person. Tilden took them round the house and afterwards showed them the grounds. He said if ever any of it could be used for the benefit of the mining community he would be pleased to discuss any proposition put forward.

They went round a big wooden building which we came to know as "The Barn" and the large meadow at the back of the house, which became the Officials Cricket Pitch. In a moment of conversation, Tilden did make the telling comment "that to achieve optimum productivity it was necessary to have a contented workforce, and this he hoped to achieve".

Before parting, Tilden said he understood the difficulties Billy faced in his position as union secretary and that he didn't wish to compromise his position, but whatever their differences they might endeavour to treat each other with mutual respect. He expressed the wish that they might meet again soon, if not individually possibly accompanied by the chairman or with other members of the committee. Tilden felt that such a meeting would be to everyone's advantage. On this basis they parted and at Billy's request the chauffeur drove Billy and his wife to Shepherdswell Station where they caught the train back to Dover.

Billy arranged a meeting with the chairman and the committee of the Union, and told them of his meeting with

Tilden, and put forward the proposition that it might be useful to arrange a visit as suggested by him. The feeling was that nothing could be lost by doing this.

They met at the mansion. Tilden gave them a warm welcome and expressed his pleasure and appreciation on meeting members of the committee. He opened the meeting by saying that his intention was to have a general discussion so that they could get to know each other. "Wages depended on productivity and profitability," and best results could not be achieved with a "dissatisfied workforce". His belief was that the colliery would be best served if a practical working relationship were to be established between "workers and management". If such a situation could be introduced, all sides would benefit.

He recognised that the function of the Union was to fight and serve the interests of its members, and that at the moment the Unions were going through a very difficult time and that there existed a wide gap between the management and the union. This, he suggested, was due to the national policy of the owners supported by the government and the aggressive attitude that the previous management had displayed toward the Union.

The government policy of privatisation and the clamour for wage cuts had provoked intense hostility among the workforce. These were national problems which unfortunately often touched on local issues. If there were any local concerns relating to the workers at Tilmanstone Colliery Tilden would do his best to help in finding solutions beneficial to all.

A number of questions were asked by members of the committee, mostly about the provision of information relating to management policy, the nature of that information and its credibility. The meeting closed with Tilden suggesting that it would prove useful if they could all meet again soon to discuss more detailed concerns, especially with the prospect of a general strike being called in the near future. The officers of the Union said they would seriously consider such a proposal as a matter of urgency, thanked Mr Tilden Smith for his hospitality and departed.

Nationally the gap between the owners and the colliers remained still as wide as ever. The feelings expressed toward management grew even more hostile. There was a genuine feeling of bitterness and growing resentment among the workforce. However several meetings were held with Mr Tilden Smith and representatives of his management, formally and informally, in early 1925 and 1926, to discuss some of the possible consequences of the proposed general strike.

He realised that the local miners would have to support their national representatives and withdraw their labour. This was a national strike, not a local dispute. He realised it would be a hard and bitter struggle, but the strike would at some time come to an end and he did not wish to have a dissatisfied workforce on his hands when the men returned to work.

He made it clear that this situation was none of his making. He would use his good offices in an endeavour to ameliorate any suffering that might occur. He was preparing for the day when the miners would return to work and the strike over. It was with these thoughts in mind that Tilden carried on talks with Billy Newman and his Committee.

The Spirit of Respect and Trust built up by Tilden. 1925-30.
During this surprisingly short period of time, there had been a noticeable change in the attitude of the management. Gone was their aggressive manner. Though firm and business like in dealing with the Union, they were willing to listen and even discuss matters of mutual concern. However, there was still a great divide between the two sides. On the part of the Union there was still a deal of mistrust.

The union representatives were intelligent and independent minded. What mattered to them was whether their demands were met. They were not boss's men. The working relationship that had been established was fragile, and was in danger of being wrecked by the hostile attitude of government toward the miners and their determination to cut wages.

Talks were not enough. Nationally there was a growing impatience amongst the work-force with their leadership. The call was for immediate and direct action. The cry was, "Not a Penny off the Pay, Not an Hour off the Day!" This became the battle-cry. The Union had the solid support of the work-force at Tilmanstone Colliery. Emotions ran high! There was a growing feeling that the Miners National Executive should do something now!

Tilden, resilient as ever in the face of this situation, and with his plans and concerns for the future in mind, endeavoured to maintain contacts with his work-force. He met the union secretary both formally and informally on a number of occasions. They talked of the impending strike and its possible consequences. When the men were called out they would receive no wages. National union funds were insufficient to meet out of pocket expenses and ensure that mining families did not go hungry.

The committee of the Union at Tilmanstone had realised the difficulties that the families would have to face during the strike. Funds were short and with no pay families would find it very hard, perhaps impossible to meet their bills. Some shops would not serve striking miners. Even the few shopkeepers who were sympathetic to the miners and their cause found they had not the resources to grant credit. "It was pay up or you can't have it!"

Provision had to be made to ameliorate any suffering that might occur. Preparations were made to establish "soup kitchens". Collecting points were organised for receiving food parcels given by people sympathetic to the miners and their cause. Food parcels were even sent from Russia to the secretariat of Tilmanstone Colliery. Billy Newman with some comrades were photographed outside River Co-op collecting food parcels.

They were hard times and Tilden responded to this most serious situation with the proposition that he was willing to help by donating £100 a week to the union funds at Tilmanstone, on the clear understanding, that the money was to be used to relieve hardship among the wives and children of the miners, and for no other purpose. The proposition was taken back to the committee as a matter of urgency and it was agreed to accept the offer, "an open ended offer with no strings attached".

Chapter 28

The state of affairs prior to 1926.

The unrest in the mines had been on-going. It had been growing in intensity before 1914. However, it abated during the Great War of 1914, when a spirit of patriotism swept through the country. The mines were nationalised and the miners did their part in the early days of the war as volunteers, joining the army in droves to fight for King and Country. Those who remained behind, mostly the older men, did their part in the pits providing the coal necessary to fuel the war-machine.

After four long tragic years of war peace was declared but victory celebrations were tempered by expressions of war weariness. Disputes erupted in the mining industry and many broke into scenes of open hostilities with the owners who were determined in their desire to reduce costs by cutting wages and increasing hours of the working miners.

The intense feeling of anger amongst the miners was further influenced by the general unrest throughout the country. The mutiny of soldiers at various places across the country, including locally at Folkestone and Dover. Strikes took place among the police force in London, and elsewhere.

The government made known it's support of the owners and their demands. This angered the working people even more. Many workers in the dockers' and the railwaymen's unions came out and urged members of their executives to adopt a more militant approach toward the owners and government. Not all members of the union executives were in favour of such direct action. They were willing to talk but not to act. This is corroborated in Beatrice Webb's diaries. There was a distinct lack of unity among the leadership which had played a great part in the defeat of the unions in the earlier strike of 1921 when the miners were forced to go back to work under contracts decided by the owners. This defeat deeply affected the working miners and further fuelled their bitterness and anger.

The dissatisfaction of the working miners, with their conditions at work was as strong as ever. Unrest grew among the face workers. During the years of 1922, 23 and 24 there were frequent local walk-outs by militant miners. A number of local disputes occurred at Tilmanstone due to the desire of the management to crush the Union. Lead by Billy Newman, secretary and Jack Evans, the chairman, and fully supported by the committee, which included the committed communist Jackie Crane and chairman of the local branch Labour Party Bill Roome, bitter confrontation broke out between the Union and the management. At local level the men were better organised and prepared than those at national level. Little was being done by the national leadership to prepare for any action on a national scale.

The government had a very different view of things They were preparing for full scale battle, which they expected and were determined to win. Some influential members of government, such as Winston Churchill, appeared to look forward to such a fight with relish. Coal-stocks were built up to provide for any eventuality. Volunteers were recruited to help man various public services and yet the miners' leaders did nothing. The cry for action was coming from the face workers, from the working miners at the grass-roots. There had been too much talk and too many empty promises and no results. There was mounting anger among the workers. It was time for action! But where was the recognition, the preparation by the national miners' leaders for such action? There was little sign of any!

Chapter 29

Power Moves From Region To the National Union.

Prior to 1914 the unions were organised more on a regional basis. They had not yet been integrated into a national union. There were success stories of victories for the miners in Durham and South Wales. These were fought on a regional basis in organisations where the workforce and the leadership were closely integrated. These confrontations took place between the owners and the area unions. The story of the Durham miners is well told by Sidney Webb in his book 'The Durham Miners'.

The 1914-18 war was the first war that encompassed the whole population, affecting every home in the country. The means of production were taken over or regulated by government. Industries were integrated. Organisations involved a greater degree of centralisation, and the unions began to join together on a national basis to form what they hoped would be an effective, united organisation. This became known as the National Union of Mineworkers. The same developments occurred in the railway unions and among the dockers.

These organisations were seen by many politicians as providing a possible threat to government. The unions were now placed in a situation where in any dispute they would not only be faced by the owners but also directly by the government. Such a confrontation would provide formidable problems for the unions, the consequences of which the unions at national level seemed little prepared.

The miners' strike of 1920 came just at the turning point from illusory economic prosperity to that of acknowledged depression. The miners were put off with a purely temporary advance, linked to the output of coal. The government seized the occasion of the Triple Alliance's abortive threat to strike in support of the miners in the 1920's to carry into law a new oppressive measure. "The Emergency Powers Act" was passed which legally empowered the government to break any large strike if such an action was felt to endanger national security.

The government were determined to be ready for any future conflict. They piled up large stocks of coal. An elaborate organisation was set up which divided the country into ten areas under civil commissioners, whose job was to organize "voluntary strike breaking organisations". By the time the crisis broke in 1926, everything was ready for any challenge that might arise through the actions of the trades unions.

On the Labour side, the national leadership demonstrated a mixture of inopportune pacifism and over-confidence, which produced an inexcusable lack of preparedness. At the same time well known national leaders lacked belief in their own cause. They lacked belief in their own ability to carry out such actions as might arise in any such conflict.

Divisions in the Union Leadership.
The personnel of the General Council had changed, moving from left to right with the election of J.H. Thomas from the Railwaymen's Union, Arthur Pugh made president and Sir Walter Citrine the general secretary of the TUC. It was known from private conversations, recorded in Beatrice Webb's Diaries, that many of the general council were dubious about any form of strike action. There was a division of opinion among members of the general council of the TUC but they voted to reaffirm their support for the miners in spite of the fact that many of their number had reached the conclusion that a cut in wages was inevitable.

Despite all omens the Labour leaders were surprised when the conflict actually came. The Labour leaders in the words of Thomas, "begged and pleaded, almost grovelling" to members of government to find a way out, but to no avail. The government and owners were adamant and on Friday, the last day of April 1926, lock-out notices were put into effect.

At this most critical time, any shrewd observer would have formed the conclusion that here was a strong army of fearless resolute workers, determined of purpose, but virtually leaderless. There were the likes of A.J. Cook, a great orator but offering little practical vision. The Webbs recorded that many of the general council appeared to lack the confidence in themselves and were bewildered at the great crisis they had brought about. The question was were they capable of running such an operation?

My father, acquainted with many of these people, was well aware of the situation and viewed such expressions of the leadership with great concern. He was of a mind that there were weaknesses on both sides and that solidarity, unity and resoluteness of purpose expressed by the workforce might yet win the day. The strike, having been called, there was no other way but to stick with the federation. Billy was of the opinion that even at this juncture any division would do nothing except make matters worse. To maintain the spirit of unity, the belief in the rightness of their cause and to build a high morale among the workers and their families it was necessary to work together and act together. This was now the priority.

The Kent coalfield consisted of 4 pits, Tilmanstone, Snowdown, Chislet and Betteshanger. The unions came together to form the Kent Miners' Federation. Billy Newman, secretary of Tilmanstone, became president of the Kent Miners' Association in 1922 and remained in that office throughout the 1926 Strike until the year 1933, some twelve years later. The workforce in all these pits were united in their action during the crisis of 1926, in which Billy Newman played a significant role. The committee members and the Union secretaries of the different pits did all they could in support of their workforce. The activists held varied and strong political allegiances to the left of the political spectrum. There were Communists, members of the ILP and the main stream Labour Party, united in their action, all acting together, in the interests of the workers at the pits and on behalf of their families.

However there was a distinct difference of attitude in the different pits between unions and management. The fight was directed against management who were plainly seen as representing the owners and carrying out their directives. There had been troubles through-out the 1920's and the miners in all the pits in the Kent coalfield had a reputation for their extreme militancy, Tilmanstone included.

In 1925, a year before the general strike of 1926, as has already been mentioned, a great change took place at Tilmanstone Pit. The pit was taken over by a new owner, Mr Tilden Smith, who let it be known that this dispute was none of his doing.

He made it known that he understood that the miners at Tilmanstone Colliery would be expected to support the call by the National Miners Federation for a general strike and that the pit would close, but he hoped that in the long run, it would not endanger the good relations between union and management which he hoped to build up. Tentative lines of communication were established and relations with management began to improve. It was made plain to Mr Tilden Smith that words were not enough. There had been too much talk and too many broken promises. Actions were needed to demonstrate that any words uttered were meaningful, not just hollow, empty expressions.

As a result of the approaches made by Mr Tilden Smith to the union leaders, the action at Tilmanstone was deflected from action against the local management and directed against the government who, acting in collusion with the owners nationally, were intent on increasing hours and cutting wages. The men at Tilmanstone, as resolute and as militant as ever, continued to give full support to their workers nationally, with their slogan, "Not a minute off the Day, Not a Penny off the Pay".

Chapter 30

1926 The Strike.

The government was facing the greatest civil crisis of the times. The government and the owners were adamant and on Friday, the last day of April 1926, "lock-out notices went into effect". The result of this action was that the division within the Union leadership was made public. It injected fire and backbone into some leaders, whilst others sought peace at any price.

Ernest Bevin, who had been a moderating influence during the early discussions, had no doubt as to how the Unions should respond to the challenge. It was the TUC's duty to "fight for the soul of Labour and the salvation of the miners". The owners refused to withdraw the lock-out notices and the general strike began at one minute to midnight on 3rd. May 1926.

The first and most powerful battalions to come out on the Monday were "the transport workers of every kind, sea, land and air." When the bells rang out at midnight on Monday over the silent cities they announced the beginning of a stillness which nobody had ever known before in English history. This was a revelation to all involved and demonstrated the true power and might of the workers when acting together. This was the greatest confrontation between the combined force of the unions and the owners, and one which with a clear sense of unity on behalf of the leadership of the TUC and between the miners' leaders might have resulted in a successful conclusion, instead it ended in complete disaster.

The general strike itself, lasted a little less than 9 days. The leaders of the general council of the TUC, led by the chairman, Arthur Pugh, and by the secretary, Walter Citrine, on Wednesday, May 12 1926 issued the statement which read, "That the general strike is to be called off forthwith." J.H. Thomas of the Railwaymen's Union commented that his colleagues had done "the big thing".

It was over for the leaders perhaps, but not for the rank and file workers. For some time the workers stayed out. The newspapers did not appear, nor did the trams, trains or buses run until certain concessions were made. The general workforce had to be induced to accept decisions made on their behalf before they would return to work. The miners soon found themselves left on their own to fight by themselves.

The miners continued their struggle, which dragged on, not for a week or a month, but for another 6 months. In spite of their suffering, most of the working miners remained solid in support of their union and of the National Miners' Federation, which became known as the National Union of Mineworkers.

Their cry continued, "Not an hour off the day! Not a penny off the Pay!"

The government and the owners were adamant that these claims were unacceptable and insisted there must be wage cuts and an increase in hours worked. The miners were determined to carry on with their fight. It was not until November that the executive of the Miners' Federation called off the strike.

The miners after 6 months struggle were exhausted and could continue no longer. They had to accept defeat and admit that nothing whatever had been achieved.

This had been the greatest effort the British workers had ever made but a defeat after such an epic struggle took its toll on the trades union movement. Across the country trade union membership fell and it became clear that the leaders on the general council would never be able to call upon the same loyalty and sacrifice again.

The Conservative government took their revenge in 1927 by introducing 'The Trade's Disputes and Trade Union Act'. General strikes and sympathetic strikes were forbidden under clauses of widest and loosest drafting. Support for the Labour Party was weakened by making it law that any member of the Union who wished to make a donation to the Labour Party had to request to do so. Severe penalties were prescribed and fresh restrictions on picketing were enacted.

Locally the Unions of the East Kent coalfield had been very active, keeping support of their members. By working closely with the striking miners and their families they had been able to keep the support of most of the workforce and maintain a high state of morale in spite of the great amount of suffering they had to endure. The workmen at Tilmanstone were part of this force, part of the East Kent coalfield.

The struggle had lasted 6 months and the executive of the Miners' Federation felt that the workmen, and their families, had suffered enough. They had given their all and could not be asked to make more sacrifices. It was then that notices were issued by the national executive stating that the strike should end and men return to work.

At Tilmanstone this notice was received with mixed feeling. A proud workforce who had endured so much and fought their cause with such vigour, to admit defeat was something they found hard to accept. All their efforts it seemed had come to no avail.

The men expressed their feelings in different ways. Many were bitter and resentful, others were pleased to be back at work, taking home a pay packet to provide once more for their family. There were gatherings of miners in the pubs, on the street corners and in the Labour halls, all discussing the situation which they felt difficult to grasp.

What was to happen next? Would they be blacklisted? What hours would they have to work? Would their wages be cut? These thoughts were uppermost in the minds of the miners and their families. They were deeply concerned! They were worried and anxious!

For those few hours after the announcement many felt isolated, on their own, not knowing what the future held for them, and their families. They joined together seeking the latest information. At Tilmanstone the union secretary distributed notices with the latest news, and plans for meetings to be held and discuss any concerns union members might have. Many of the miners were worried that the Union could not now offer them any protection, and so, they waited!

Back To Work.

At last a Notice was issued by the management at Tilmanstone and posted in various places including the surrounding villages.

Tilmanstone Colliery.

"This pit is open for work on terms posted at the colliery, and signing on for an immediate resumption of work may be made on Monday morning, the 15th. November 1926.

"Persons employed at this colliery prior to the stoppage are given 24 hours from 5.30 am on Monday 15th November, to sign on, otherwise they will not be guaranteed to be taken on again.

By Order."

The terms to which the notice referred, were posted at the Colliery. The notice and terms were reported to a meeting which was held in the Eythorne Cinema on the Sunday morning called by the secretary, Billy Newman. He was a man of strong conviction and with a firm belief in the justness of the miners' cause, but in terms of action, he was very much a pragmatist. This had been a national strike and lacking the necessary support in the rest of the country, and without the backing of the National Miners' Federation, no purpose would be served by continuing the strike. He felt there was no alternative but to accept the decision of the federation.

There was a great deal of heated discussion with some members in favour of carrying on the strike. Toward the end of the meeting a resolution was put that they "Stand by the decision of the federation and return to work". This was carried by an overwhelming majority.

However the procedures laid down by the management for a return to work were issues of major contention. There was a great deal of concern relating to the time limit of 24 hours. It was felt that it would be impossible for many workers to be ready for work in that space of time. Billy Newman immediately contacted the management and obtained a stay of a further 24 hours. The final date for signing-on was deferred until 5.30 on the Wednesday morning.

A full meeting of the Union was called on the Tuesday evening.

The hall was packed with busloads of miners arriving from Dover. There was much debate and the men expressed many different and sometimes heated views. They were very angry. The meeting was finally addressed by the secretary and chairman and it was decided that the men be recommended to sign-on by the Wednesday morning.

Upward of 700 men signed-on and work commenced at the colliery with the night shift on Wednesday night. Mr Newman, is described by Mr Sherren in his book, 'Industrial Eden' as "a very strong union secretary".

Chapter 31

The Turbulent Times and Division among the Leadership.

These were turbulent times when, in the year 1919, Billy, aged 34, was thrust into the challenging and uncertain world of local union and Labour Party politics. The national leaders were a mixed and varied group of individuals. Some such as Ernie Bevin and A.J. Cook were primarily union men. Others, such as Manny Shinwell and Ramsay McDonald, saw their role primarily as politicians, and then, there were people like Jimmy Thomas who felt that they had an important part to play in both, but appeared to be more at home in the plush ministerial offices in Downing Street than mixing with their fellow union bosses. I mention these personalities since they, with others, played a major role in the confrontational struggles between the government and the trades unions in the 1920's, leading to the almost annihilation of the unions as a result of the gross failure of 'their leadership' during the 1921 and the 1926 national strikes.

Some commentators, and historians, may feel that to accord such comments, which infer such a severe degree of culpability on these national representatives, as somewhat harsh. They may be right but to the likes of my father, a working miner, giving his all to persuade his fellow workers to make such enormous sacrifices, involving themselves, their wives and children, he felt that they deserved better.

Many of the leaders kept their position. They kept their status! The men at the coal face lost a great deal and many lost everything. Billy Newman agreed more with the assertions of Beatrice Webb written in her diaries commenting on the earlier struggles of the 1921 strike, I quote "April 16th 1921... 'The strike cancelled' was the staggering news headline of yesterday's evening paper". This day became known as Black Friday, when after a compromising speech by the leader of the miners Frank Hodges the leaders of the other unions, who had come out in support of the miners, went back to work leaving the miners to fight on their own. Frank Hodges resigned his position as the General Secretary of the Miners Union as the men continued with their strike action.

This division of ranks and the break-up of the Triple Alliance was recognised as a disastrous defeat and a severe blow to morale among members of the trades union movement. Clearly the aspiration of solidarity was not sufficiently shared by the leadership of the unions. As Beatrice Webb writes, "the leaders clearly funked it: Thomas, Bevin, and even Williams together with a majority of the executives of the NUR and Transport Workers rode off, on the refusal of the Miners' Executive, to ratify Hodges unauthorised offer on behalf of the miners in private conversation with the government".

Beatrice Webb says, "There is something strangely ludicrous in these unauthorised friendly talks with the capitalist government and the capitalist MPs after all the tall talk about 'the enemy'. These Labour leaders are the limit of inconsequence: ready to be hail-fellow-well-met at one moment with any casual minister or MP, - not omitting the Prime Minister - and at another time denouncing these same men as the Mammon of Unrighteousness whom they are out to destroy. As for Thomas, he feels himself at home in Downing Street rather than among noxious competitors in a Trade Union Conference. - The manual workers cannot find men of sufficient character and intellect to lead them in the higher ranges of statesmanship. That is the plain truth."

"April 24th... The gossip of Ecclestone Square throws no further light on the great strike fiasco. Thomas and Bevin had from the first objected to the Triple Alliance Strike and Thomas had been intriguing with other parties to prevent it. Hodges knew on the Thursday night that Thomas and Co. intended to call off the strike... One of the worst features of this ludicrous and tragic business was the failure in loyalty of these men to each other!! Clynes, the leader of the Parliamentary Labour Party, was left to make his speech in Parliament on Friday afternoon in total ignorance of the cancelling of the strike, when the front bench, the government, knew every latest detail. They had been informed by Thomas... I wonder when these men will ever learn the elements of Good Comradeship!"

It was against this background of intrigues and petty jealousies at the heart of the leadership of the trades union movement, magnified by the spread of misinformation, gossip and rumour that local officials, such as my father as secretary of the Tilmanstone Miners Union, were expected to make relevant judgements and to act.

Chapter 32

Tilden Smith and the Union.
Dr. George Bell.

Dr George Bell, Dean of Canterbury Cathedral. 1927

From 1919 to 1924 the policy of local management was to crush the Union. The tactics of the management were those of confrontation. There was an absolute refusal by the management to negotiate on any issue. Billy Newman and his committee, with the full support of the membership, decided to accept the challenge and fight back.

In 1925, the colliery was taken over by Mr Tilden Smith and during his time as the owner of Tilmanstone Colliery the relationship between the Union and management changed completely from one of confrontation to one of close and lasting co-operation. "How and in what circumstances did this come to pass in such a short period of time, 1925 to 1930, when in so many parts of the country, labour relations were in such turmoil?"

Mr Sherren in his excellent account of the development of Tilmanstone Colliery, gives great credit for this change to Tilden Smith, and deservedly so. He was a man of imagination, shrewd of mind who believed that such a change was not only desirable but vitally necessary if his plans for the pit and the surrounding area of east Kent were to succeed. The one thing he needed was continuity of production.

He approached such changes as he deemed necessary with determination. Time was of the essence.

Tilden took a hands on approach to the strategic management of the pit, appointing an excellent area manager, Mr Victor Hare, a general manager, Mr Bernard Whitaker, and Mr David Jenkins as cashier, who in today's terminology would be known as the chief finance officer. These men proved themselves to have both skills in management and real expertise in particular areas of mining.

When Tilden took over the colliery the workforce was well known for its extreme militancy. The Union representatives had no trust in the management. The situation between 1919 and 1924 had been one of continual and fierce conflict which did not change on the arrival of Tilden Smith. Why should it? Tilden Smith had been associated with the colliery since he first tried to gain control as early as 1915 when his efforts were thwarted by Arthur Burr. In the eyes of the miners at Tilmanstone he was associated with the likes of Arthur Burr and his policies during the troubled times of 1919 - 1924.

Whatever his ambitions, the arrival of Tilden brought no immediate change in the relationship between the management and the workforce. However, as owner he had the power to bring about such change and he had the confidence that with the right approach he could accomplish that change. He needed to build up trust between himself, the union officials and the workforce. He used his imagination, his great experience in negotiations and was not above using subterfuge to bring it about. He wanted to establish a spirit of co-operation between management and the unions, a seemingly impossible project at that time. Distrust of the management appeared so entrenched in the minds of the union officials that nothing could alter their feelings.

That there would be a turn round in attitude and approach in such a short space of time, and a working relationship of remarkable unity achieved, was to be a kind of progress unparalleled in the history of coal-mining.

The main personalities that such a change so much depended on were of course Tilden Smith, the owner of the Pit, and Billy Newman who held the vital positions of Secretary of the Tilmanstone Miners Union, President of the East Kent Miners Association and Chairman of the Dover District Labour Party. He was a man of some power and influence in the district.

At this juncture Billy Newman saw no reason why the unions, expressly militant in their attitude toward the owner and management, should in any way change. He was not prepared to let his guard down. Tilden Smith may have had no direct involvement in the actions of the management in the troublesome years of 1919-1924, but it was known that he had financial interests in Tilmanstone Colliery. To people like Billy Newman why should things be any different now than they had been in the past years. He and his committee refused to consider any overtures made on Tilden's behalf to have talks with the Union except on an official basis.

Feelers were put out by Tilden to try and ease the tension between the two sides. At various important functions Billy Newman found himself as a guest at which Tilden Smith was present along with other men of influence and good-will.

One such occasion was a meeting at Canterbury Cathedral of the Institute of Town Planning as early as 1925, where Billy Newman found himself a guest of honour seated in the centre of the front row in a photo-shoot with the Dean of Canterbury, The Rev Dr George Bell, and of course Tilden Smith, Lord Northbourne and many other persons of power and influence in East Kent.

George Bell   Billy   Tilden

One afternoon Henrietta Bell invited my father and mother to their residence at Canterbury Cathedral to join them for tea. During the afternoon Dr Bell took father on a tour of the cathedral grounds. It was a bright, sunny day, and Billy Newman could not but be impressed by the beauty and magnificence of the cathedral and in such splendid grounds. They talked of family and work, and labour relations at the pit.

As the warm sun came shining through the trees whilst admiring a beautiful rose, father was so overcome by the beauty of the scene he immediately expressed his thoughts with the words, "My! What a lovely place this is! It must be wonderful to live and work here, it's so peaceful."

As Dr Bell turned to him, Billy saw a tear roll down Dr Bell's cheek. "Yes Newman!" he said and paused, and then continued almost sadly, "You know! There are thorns even here!" and after a moment of quiet reflection, he added, "but this is a place of great grandeur and glory. It holds a tradition of deep spiritual belief and a sense of great hope for the future of mankind," and that genial smile was back again. My father turned to me, and said, "Son, this meeting introduced me to one of the most remarkable men it has ever been my lot to meet!"

The relationship between these two men based upon what might be seen as a chance meeting of two people thrown together by the problems of the time developed into a lifelong friendship. Dr Bell would often meet with father. They enjoyed each other's company and would discuss matters of common interest. Conversation included the day to day practical problems of the mining community, but often ventured into the more philosophic speculations of life in general, and of course talk of family concerns.

It appears strange that Dr Bell, educated at Oxford, a friend and associate of the likes of R.H. Tawney, and members of what might be called the Establishment, should be quite at home with the working class Billy Newman, who left school at 13, and was very much a product of the rough and tumble of the backstreets.

In spite of the difference in social background there was a great similarity between the two men in terms of their intellect and purpose in life, as manifest in the manner of their thought and expression.

During his stay at Canterbury, The Reverend Dr George Bell was a frequent visitor to our home at Eythorne. I remember, aged 4 or 5, going into the room, which we knew as dad's office, to ask if they were ready for tea. Present were my father, Dr Bell, white collar, black waistcoat and strange black trousers with gaiters and a young lady called Miss Phyllian, a social worker, who was then working as a warden at Elvington Settlement. Dr Bell looked at me and asked me what I wanted to do when I grew up?

My reply was to go on the dole, I wouldn't have to work then! Miss Phyllian came to my rescue to prevent me possibly being reprimanded by my father. Her comment, "Leave the poor lad alone, I thought that was a very good answer young man. Go and tell your mother that we are ready for tea."

The next time I met Dr Bell was when I was about 18. Father and I drove down to Chichester. We stayed the night at an old inn that had just become a Trust House. It was situated opposite Chichester Cathedral. The next day, which was a bright sunny day, we walked along the river to the Bishop's Palace where we were greeted by Mrs Bell. She took us in the house but said that she didn't know whether Dr Bell would be able to see us because he was entertaining a number of students intending to join the clergy. On being informed of our arrival Dr Bell left his charges and came to greet us. He then took us to meet his guests and after a brief conversation with father, we parted and went on our way.

Dr Bell was a great influence in bringing Tilden Smith into a closer relationship with my father. This factor contributed a great deal to the change in the nature of governance at Tilmanstone Colliery.

The years of 1919 to 1925, ones of militant confrontation, changed in a surprisingly short space of time, under Tilden, to one of trust and co-operation.

Chapter 33

Wyndham Deedes and the Elvington Settlement.

The second unlikely figure to play a part in cementing this good relationship between management and the Union was Brigadier Sir Wyndham Deedes.

A great deal of work was done by those employed by the National Council of Social Services under the guidance of Brigadier Sir Wyndham Deedes. The Council was initially a voluntary organisation funded by men of goodwill. Wyndham Deedes was its secretary in the 20s' and 30's until the outbreak of war in 1939.

Wyndham Deedes was of a well-known family living in Hythe. As a schoolboy he attended Eton and then joined the Army. The mayoral notice board in the town hall of Hythe contains the names of a number of his family. He was a person of some influence in the area.

He served in South Africa, Libya, and in the Middle East. During the first world war he took part in landings at Gallipoli. He became a brigadier general and was highly thought of in military circles, later serving as chief secretary to Herbert Samuel, High-Commissioner of Palestine and then with the Governor of Malta.

At first instance he appeared the most unlikely person that I thought of as being sympathetic to the welfare of the working class or the miners' cause. However, it was in fact Sir Wyndham Deedes who was instrumental in setting up the Elvington Miners' Settlement.

At a meeting which took place at the Mary Ward Settlement it was proposed that a settlement should be established in a coal mining district. The idea was later in the year pursued at Cambridge House. By this time negotiations had already started with Tilden Smith, owner of Tilmanstone Coal Mine in Kent.

By February 1927 the first contribution of £100 from the Kent Coalfields Company was received, and it was agreed to put a rent free cottage for use by the Settlement Council. A woman warden was appointed to be in charge of what was described of as "this pioneering enterprise".

A meeting was soon held consisting of those immediately concerned with the project and the Dean of Canterbury, Dr George Bell took the chair. Later in 1927, an AGM was held chaired by Mr H. E. Rice, at which the functions of the Settlement were set out by Sir Wyndham Deedes and an election of local representatives took place.

Due to the work of Sir Wyndham Deedes, Dr George Bell and Tilden, with the support of Billy Newman, Union Secretary, the first such settlement was established at the mining village of Elvington. Those showing interest included, The Womens Institute (95) members, Infant Welfare (63), Choral Society (27), Home Nursing (14), Folk Dancing (17), Tennis Club (50), Library (186), Ambulance Class (33), Play Centre (70).

The warden was Miss Jan McDonald. The council elected to support her were the Dean of Canterbury, Dr George Bell, Dr Bellamy, Mr W. Newman (representing the miners), Mr Bernard Whittaker (manager of Tilmanstone Colliery), Mr Edward Rice and the Hon. Walter James, etc. The aim was to create an active and vibrant community.

Over a period of time, the wardens changed. They were

mostly young lady graduates from the universities. The Settlement proved a success.

I well remember the names of those who came to the house either on a social visit or seeking information from my father on matters of community welfare. They had a flat at the Elvington Settlement, but would often come and join us for tea. Most of them became friends and remained in touch with the family for many years after they had left the area. The names I remember include Miss Jan McDonald, a graduate of London School of Economics, who had previously worked in a library in Jerusalem when Wyndham Deedes worked with the Governor of Palestine, Miss Ruth Bowley, Miss Griggs, Miss Mabel Phyllian of Manchester who was later known as Dr Tylecote and became Lord Mayor of Manchester. Then there was Miss Barbara Murray, who from 1933, worked with Sir Wyndham helping refugees escape from Nazi Germany and Miss Leek who devoted much of her life helping children in southern Africa.

They were dedicated workers with a variety of talent. They would often visit the house to see whether there was a cup of tea on the table. Mother was always welcoming, treating them like members of the family.

Sometimes they would come when union members and local dignitaries were present including the doctor, the vicar, or the headmaster, Mr George Cook. These ad-hoc meetings would develop into the discussion of concerns that confronted those who lived in the village. There was a to and fro of ideas.

These gatherings were veritable seminars of a very high level. The discussions even ranged into questions of the crisis looming on the horizon, particularly the rise of the Nazi Party in Germany. Miss Phyllian, a frequent visitor to Germany and Austria, was very well informed of the state of affairs in those countries. This was at a time when the WEA was flourishing and, with Victor Gollancz as publisher, the Left Wing Bookclub was being established. Many experiences and ideas were exchanged, and much was learned by all, to the great benefit of the community. It was a great school of learning.

Chapter 34

Tilden and the Union. Community Activities. The Russian Visit.

In a short space of time relations between the Union and the owner, Mr Tilden Smith, became a co-operative and trusted relationship, and all those living at Elvington and working at Tilmanstone Colliery benefited. Tilden was pleased to allow his mansion and grounds to be used for community purposes and miners functions. 'The Barn' was converted for use as a community hall where concerts and dances took place.

Functions were held in attempts to bring the various facets of the communities together. These were the well-established residents of Eythorne and the miners who had settled at Elvington.

The concerts drew on local talent which the miners and their families possessed to a remarkable degree. A lively and flourishing amateur dramatics group was formed under the direction of a Mrs Clout of Dover, which included members from both Elvington and Eythorne. They worked closely with the staff and pupils of Elvington Elementary School and were well known for the their excellent and regular performances. Mr Day, the headmaster gave all possible support.

The miner's choir, Tilmanstone Male Voice Choir, like those of the other pits became well-known throughout the district and besides singing locally it was in demand to perform in many town concert halls in Kent. They were a familiar sight at all the concerts in the Barn and Elvington Community Centre. Miners were particularly rich in musical talent and dance bands flourished.

The grounds behind the mansion included a large meadow surrounded by trees which was converted into a cricket pitch used by the officials of the colliery. A cricket match was annually organised with the miners team playing the officials. Sometimes a fete was held at the same time.

I remember attending such a match just before the outbreak of war, 1938. It was a bright summer's day and ice-cream stalls were conveniently situated and did a flourishing trade. It so happened that on that day the Test Match between England and Australia was being played. We, of course, were watching the Miners v. Officials match, all very impressively dressed in their whites.

Tilmanstone male voice choir presented with a cup by leader of the Labour Party, George Lansbury.

Suddenly play stopped, and there was a rush to some cars which had fitted the latest radio sets. There was complete silence. The young Len Hutton was batting and was about to make Test history by achieving the highest score in a Test match with Australia that had yet been made, 361. The score was announced and the silence broken with a mighty cheer. Lunch was announced after which play was started again. The miners' match was resumed. Incidentally it was at this Test match that the young Dennis Compton first played for England. It was a wonderful day and a good time was had by all.

So well had Tilden Smith cemented a sense of trust between himself, the management and the Miners Union that many of the joint activities that he encouraged and promoted lasted long after his unfortunate death in 1930.

Lord Northbourne, George Lansbury and Billy Newman.

During that short space of time, 1925 to 1930, he gave much more to the life of the mining community than anyone could ever have imagined. In co-operation with my father as both Secretary of the Union and Chairman of the Dover District Labour Party, invitations were made to eminent Labour figures to come as guests and address the miners at fetes organised in his grounds. George Lansbury, then leader of the Labour Party, was one such guest. Most importantly, for the first time a management committee was set up which included a representative of the Miners Union who played a full part in decision making at Tilmanstone Colliery.

Tilden was adept at the way he gained the confidence of people who were at first very distrustful of what his objectives were and what he, as owner of Tilmanstone Colliery, intended.

During the early years of the 1920's, before Tilden took

over, there had developed a great deal of animosity verging on enmity between the workmen and the bosses. To bridge this gap seemed an almost impossible task, given the breadth of the divide. Tilden with his experience, imagination and ingenuity managed to do just that.

One example of such action is the well documented account of the time he paid and organised a visit by two working miners, to the mining area of the Soviet Union, to gain first-hand experience of the working methods in the Russian communist coal mines.

The miners involved were Mr Jackie Crane, a committed communist, and Mr Bill Roome of the Labour Party.

Their visit was to coal mines in the Donnetz Basin. They went underground and experienced the severe conditions in which the Soviet miners worked. They found that the conditions of work at Tilmanstone Colliery were far superior to those in the mines they visited in the Soviet Union. The harsh conditions they had to endure while working in Stalin's Russia caused them to change their attitude to Mr Tilden Smith and his attempts to break down barriers to negotiations between himself and the Union and build up a spirit of co-operation. However they remained committed members of their respective political parties.

Tilden was not above carrying out acts of subterfuge which is well illustrated as when he arranged his first meeting with Billy Newman, the union secretary. He left a message at the pit asking him immediately after work, to call at the mansion where his wife was waiting for him.

Tilden later apologised for having taken such an action and hoped it caused no real inconvenience, but thought it of prime importance that they should meet. He impressed upon my father that there were matters to be discussed which were of deep concern to management, to the Union and workforce. Initially these matters were to ensure that all were informed of the general aims of future management and the relationship he hoped to establish with the Union. He wished that Billy as union secretary should be aware of the path he intended to follow. He did not expect any conclusions to be reached on a personal basis at this meeting, but hoped that as a result of their meeting, some attempt be made on a formal basis following official union procedure to discuss matters of common concern.

During this time Billy found himself a guest at many important functions either through the instigation of Tilden or Dr Bell, the Dean of Canterbury.

Billy and his wife were guests at the wedding of Mr Rice and Lord Curzon's daughter, attending their wedding in London and later at a grand reception at Mr Rice's mansion in Tilmanstone village. The Rice family owned much of the land surrounding the colliery and received royalties where tunnels were dug and coal extracted from beneath their land. Lady Curzon was the daughter of the wealthy Lord Curzon who at one time had been a minister in government serving as Foreign Secretary. They were a powerful family, well known members of the aristocracy, with properties in London.

From odd comments that my father made and photos I possess it is obvious that a mutual respect and friendly relationship grew up between my father and Mr Tilden Smith and that their discussions went well beyond the formal and official matters. They gave to my father an insight into the man's thinking. Talking one afternoon whilst relaxing over a cup of tea, taking a rest from entertaining his more affluent guests, my father commented on Tilden's power and wealth, and said, "It must feel very gratifying to have such power and wealth, to be such a rich man!".

Tilden replied, "Newman, you are the truly rich man. Just look round at all my wealthy associates. Newman, if I lost all my money, none of these would be here. Few would acknowledge me, and yet you with little money and no wealth, when you walk along the road everybody you pass greets you with a friendly word and a cheerful smile. That's what real richness is, and you've got it!"

Again, a comment that displays an inner doubt, a touch of scepticism about the nature of humanity.

Tilden was talking to Billy's brother, a fervent Salvationist, about obtaining tickets to a grand concert being given by the Salvation Army at the Albert Hall. He asked Uncle Dick, who was an officer in the Salvation Army, if he would be going. The reply was "No. There was no room, all the tickets were gone. It was a sell-out."

Tilden said, "I'll get you one if you would like to go." Dicks' reply was that Tilden could not possibly get a ticket. If the Salvation Army said they were sold out that would be the truth, it was a matter of principle.

Tilden replied that given the right price it is surprising what you can buy! Dick still held to his position, but at the end of the week Dick received two tickets, one for himself and one for his wife. This story, reminded me much of a scene in Bernard Shaw's play, 'Major Barbara.'

Whatever he may have thought of the shortcomings of some members of the Salvation Army, Tilden Smith had a great respect for the many Salvationists who did so much good work among those in need of help. This is exemplified in the case of Jabez Balfour who when released from prison went to the Salvation Army for help. Mr Tilden Smith, being made acquainted with the fact, kindly gave him assistance and employment.

Chapter 35

Visit to Essen in Germany, and the Tragic Death of Tilden Smith.

It was in 1929 when Tilden was on the verge of achieving his vision of a modern industrial complex in East Kent, that he sent a delegation from Tilmanstone Pit to Essen in Germany. Their mission was to study the latest methods of mining employed by the German mining engineers in the collieries of the Ruhr. Those in the delegation, included the Under-Manager, Mr Bramley, a Deputy and Under-ground Manager, Mr Durbin, and the Secretary of the Union, Billy Newman.

They were received in Germany by the manager of the pit Herr Binder and the secretary of the union, Herr Becker. The colliery they visited was a Krupp's Colliery, Salzer-Neuack, Essen. The date was June 26th 1929. It was at the time of great unrest in Germany with Hitler's struggle for power and the confrontations between the Nazis and the left-wing trade unionists.

Durbib	Billy Newman	Bramley	Herr Binder	Herr Becker
Deputy	Union	Under Manager	Manager	Union

In spite of this social unrest, the delegation were given a generous welcome and new friendships were made.

In terms of practical possibilities and ideas relating to the introduction of modern mining measures the visit proved most fruitful. To carry out such schemes of modernisation as witnessed in the mines of Essen was all part of Tilden's vision.

Unfortunately the great tragedy occurred, and Mr Tilden Smith collapsed on the floor of the House of Commons. His dream was not to be.

Though the plans he set, and the visions he had for East Kent, never came to fruition, much of what he did to enrich the life of the mining community in Elvington and other parts of East Kent were well established, and continued over the years to contribute to the quality of life of people living in the area. Even after Tilden's death the relationship between management and union remained one of close co-operation and in the eyes of some, it was perhaps seen as his greatest achievement during such troubled times.

Quoting from a letter of the Bishop of Chichester, Dr. Bell, to my father dated 27th December 1929,

> "I feel so sorry, especially for all at Tilmanstone and also because as you said in your letter, had Mr Tilden Smith lived he might indeed have shown the world how to solve the problem of industrial peace. I shall think constantly of you and be most grateful for any news. With Hope and Best Wishes.
> Yours very sincerely,
> George Cicestre
> G.K.A. Bell."

The comments of my father relating to industrial peace demonstrate how great a change between the management and the Union had been achieved in such a short space of time, between 1925 and 1930. The trust and respect established between these two men was indeed remarkable. Both men had clear aims and gave everything they knew to achieve those aims.

Chapter 36

Dr George Bell and My Father.

From the beginning, the association of my father with Dr George Bell seemed a most unlikely proposition and may have been put down as entirely due to chance. The more religiously inclined might have held to the maxim, "God moves in mysterious ways!" However, they did meet and from the first there developed a close friendship.

It must be remembered that Billy Newman left school at 13, and was working down the pit before the year 1897 was out, this during the time of the Boer Wars. Black with coal dust he rarely saw the light of day. He was a member of a very poor family, brought up almost entirely by his widowed mother.

George Bell, on the other hand, the younger son of a vicar was brought up in a well off, secure family at the vicarage on Hayling Island. The only thing they had in common was that they were born within a year of one another; George Bell in the year 1883, and Billy Newman in 1884.

They both lived through the many tumultuous times, witnessing momentous changing events, but these events would have been viewed by each from very different perspectives.

The Indian summer of the Victorian era was beginning to fade. In domestic politics Gladstone was mid-way through his second administration and ominous clouds were darkening the horizon, at home and abroad. Nobody could have predicted the revolutions which were to rock the foundations of European society and Christian civilisation.

They were events of such magnitude that they shook the world. They included the Great War of 1914, the Russian Revolution of 1917 and the rise of Hitler and Nazism leading to the Second World War of 1940. The systematic killing of the Gypsies, the murder of Jews in the Warsaw Ghetto and the destruction of much of European Russia with the death of millions of Russians. The policy of carpet bombing by the British, advocated by 'Bomber Harris' with the mass bombing and complete destruction of German cities. The firing and burning of Hamburg where whole families running to escape were dragged into the firestorm and burned alive.

This was not war but a horrifying perversion of all the values that European society was supposedly fighting to protect. This was followed by the complete destruction of the Japanese cities of Hiroshima and Nagasaki with the atom bomb. Families, whole populations were burnt to a cinder. This was human devastation, involving suffering on an unimaginable scale. This was not attributable to natural disasters but to the deliberate action of mankind.

It seems miraculous that in spite of such enormous human tragedy there was still a positive creative ability in the human consciousness, which demonstrated itself in the great leaps forward in science and technology. The development of the motor car and its mass production, the aeroplane and the use of nuclear energy have all, in their way, impinged upon our minds and our way of thinking.

In politics we see the rise of the Labour Party and the establishment of the Welfare State by the Attlee government of 1945. These years, during the lifetime of George Bell and Billy Newman, were indeed remarkable times; "Times of Great Change," particularly with the advent of radio and television.

Billy's early life was marked by his association with the children on the streets of the mining towns, this during the 1880s. It was a rough introduction to life in a rough and neglectful world. He was fortunate that it left him unscathed, whereas some of his young friends ended up in the hands of the police and later served many years in and out of prison. He would often tell of various boyhood incidents.

One such story that he told was of an incident that occurred on a bright Saturday morning. It was market day and the streets were crowded with people shopping, looking for a Saturday morning bargain. On passing a fruit-stall, with its bright colours reflecting the early morning sun, one of Billy's friends picked up an apple and ran. The owner spotted him and there was a hue and cry. Billy escaped, hiding behind a barrel, but some of his friends were caught and handed over to the police. A number of those boyhood friends spent many years of their lives behind bars in prison.

Billy who had escaped that first encounter with the police, often said "There but for the grace of God go I!"

During his youth he spent much of his little leisure time going to local fetes and in summer joining with his friends on bus trips to the sea-side. His friends and acquaintances were all miners like himself. Their lives even at the early age of 13 to 18 was centred round their work at the pit and their home. The theory of divine stratification still lingered on. Burke talked of "the swinish multitude".

Society was very class bound. Billy and his friends read of famous people and they talked of famous people, but they never mixed with such people.

George Bell was born to a life of what my father would have called privilege. He lived in a different world. He attended Westminster School and at the age of 18 was awarded a place at Christ Church College, Oxford. New friendships that enriched the quality of his life included meeting A.A. Milne, Sir Adrian Boult, Sir Henry Tizard at Westminster School and at Oxford he befriended William Temple, later to become Archbishop of Canterbury.

Bell had a profound interest in University Settlements and became Secretary of the Oxford Settlements Committee. He took part in the university extension movement and lectured for the WEA. George Bell was invited to become the chaplain to Archbishop Davidson. Before accepting the post he consulted Bishop Gore, Cosmo Lang and William Temple. George Bell went to join Archbishop Davidson at Lambeth Palace the very night war was declared in 1914.

George Bell - Dean of Canterbury. 1925-1930.
It was not until the early 1920s when George Bell came to live in Canterbury and with Sir Wyndham Deedes and Tilden Smith

the Elvington Settlement was established. Miss Jan MacDonald was appointed warden. It was at this time that Billy Newman came to know this amazing personality.

As previously recorded Billy, acting as secretary of the Union, found himself in a most difficult situation which if unresolved would lead to strike action at the pit. Miss Macdonald, Warden of the Settlement, suggested and persuaded Billy that the Dean, George Bell, was sympathetic to the miners' cause and that it would be a good idea to get in touch with him and seek his help. Billy felt he had nothing to lose and was reminded of some lines of a poem that he would often quote, "If hopes were dupes, fears may be liars; it may be in yon smoke concealed your comrades chase e'en now the flyers and but for you possess the field!"

However he remained unconvinced that anything could be done. Few knew or ever heard of Dr Bell's intervention in this dispute, which to the great surprise and pleasure of Billy Newman, proved successful. The local colliery management were equally surprised at the Board of Directors change of heart. The threat of strike was called off.

During his time at Canterbury Dr George Bell displayed great interest in the welfare of the workers at Tilmanstone Colliery. Billy met the Dean on numerous occasions both at Canterbury and at our home in Eythorne. When in the area he would often drop in for a chat and a cup of tea. They soon began to enjoy each other's thoughts and ideas, and the relationship fast developed into one of close friendship. On a number of occasions, besides giving his general support, he would undertake specific work on my father's behalf. One such occasion was when, during conversation, the subject of the general health of the miners and their families came up.

Billy wondered whether it would be possible to obtain some authoritative information on the effect of poor and inadequate diet on the health of local people in the mining community. Some weeks later Billy received a letter from the Dean stating that he had been gathering information from various sources relating to the topic they had been discussing and he would send him any conclusions that might be useful.

Dated the 25th April 1929, from the Deanery, Canterbury.

"As I promised a little while ago I have tried to obtain information about the physical conditions and nourishment of miners and their families living in Aylesham based on those who come as patients to the Dover hospital. The report I have received is to the following affect. A distinction is drawn between the floating and the permanent population of Aylesham. With regard to the former, the fears I had that there is considerable physical strain and hardship owing to poor feeding is correct. But most of the permanent people are, I am informed, in better state. The strain, which in some cases has been acute, has occurred through the paying back of advances to the employers and through payments on the hire purchase system for furniture. I am told that these difficulties are lessening, but there is no doubt that many have been through these things at starvation point.

As I have already told you the experience with regard to Aylesham miners at the Canterbury hospital appears to be similar."

Yours sincerely
G.K.A. Bell.

That he had a great deal of respect for Billy Newman's opinion on a variety of matters and greatly valued his judgement was manifest in the fact that he would at times send him draft outlines of proposed letters or statements he intended to make, and he would be grateful for any comments. One such letter, which I have, was concerning an article he was writing for a magazine called Kencole.

"To my friends in the coalfield, from the Dean of Canterbury.

"The Editor has asked me to write something in Kencole, before leaving Canterbury for Chichester. I very much appreciate his request and gladly obey. I have been Dean of Canterbury for just over five years; and I part with my friends in Kent with the keenest regret. Among those friends I have had the greatest happiness of counting many individual miners, some of the owners and Managers, and (I hope they will not mind my saying so) the mining community as a whole. I shall leave their neighbourhood with special feelings of affection and sorrow. But though I leave their neighbourhood they will not leave my thoughts or interest or hopes, nor I trust shall I leave theirs. I should not, need I say, choose to leave, or ask to leave, the work I have been trying to do, or the friends I have made. Certainly, I am not going to an easier job.

"A bishop's work now is harder, more exacting and more anxious in different ways; and as for the money, well, there is not much in that, I hope, for whether a man is a bishop or a dean, if he is doing his duty most of his salary goes in one way or another on his work.

"Even during the five years that I have lived in East Kent, a great deal has happened in the coalfield. There have been many changes; a great increase in population; there have been bad times, and not a few critical times. I hope that I realise something of the struggle that different sections of the mining community have gone through, including those who have come to Kent from a long distance and have had to make ends meet, pay back debts, and try to settle down. And I do not forget the anxieties of those who own the mines, have to find the money, or have responsibilities of management. It has been, and still is a hard task for all.

"Those who have allowed me to share their friendship during these years will understand me, I know, if I venture, very humbly, to express one or two of the convictions which have got themselves burnt into my mind about the whole business. Of course they are very simple convictions, but that doesn't make them untrue or out of place. I am still fairly young, but I have lived long enough to realise that the simplest truths are often the most profound; and the things which some think don't need saying do really go deepest into men's hearts. What I want to say is just this! That which makes for happiness, and the truest kind of success in life is not anything material, but something much deeper. One element in it, I am sure, is faith, in the very largest sense of the word. But I am not going to argue about that. Another element is humanity, human feeling, sympathy.

"The rank is but the guinea stamp,
    A man's a man for a' that."

"I believe that if in business, or any other relationship, we all remembered that people were human beings, with human needs and human sensibilities, that the other fellow was at bottom very much like ourselves, and deserved equal consideration, we should all get on very much better, and work and business would be not only much more humane but more interesting, and more satisfactory from all points of view. There must be humanity and consideration on both sides, mind you - to the owner and from him, and, Mr Owner, to the miner as well as from the miner. If this point of view prevails all round, the miner will get proper pay and proper housing and decent conditions of life and work, and the owner will get the willing work he wants and his full output of coal. And, if I may say so, both miners and owners will get the things they want much more successfully and much more surely through the establishment of the human spirit, than by aiming only at the thing and not caring a button about the right spirit. Some of the most useful things come after all (so we are told aren't we in coal mining) as bye-products. The right spirit, the treatment of men as human beings, is what we should aim for, and the things will follow as by-products! Only the right spirit, the human treatment, must be on both sides. There must be a determination to get rid of that terrible poison of mutual suspicion; and a willingness to trust on each side of the table; a belief in, and respect for the human nature of both.

"My readers will say that I am preaching. But that is not at all what I set out to do. What I am writing is really common sense, and a plea for common sense. There is a good deal of common sense after all in trying to get a good spirit of co-operation and humanity. And what is more the thing has been done. I know one mine in this neighbourhood (Tilmanstone) where a real effort is being made, and real success is being achieved, because real humanity is being shown on these very lines. And very great credit is due to the owner and manager and to the miners' leaders concerned. Once such a spirit is started in any mine there is no knowing how far it may go. It ought to go right through the staff and the men, and reach far beyond one particular mine. The natural conditions in Kent are so beautiful, why shouldn't the human conditions be as grand!

"I must beg my friends to forgive these remarks. I have ventured to make them, simple as they are, because I wanted to express certain of the things I feel most deeply in this business. May I say once again how very grateful I am for my friendships in the Kent Coalfield, that I shall not forget either them or it! And may I add that when I get to Sussex, after all only the next county, I shall watch developments, human, as well as economic, developments, with the greatest of interest, and that if ever I can help in any way, I shall be only too ready to do so".

G.K.A. Bell.

Dr Bell, in spite of the many concerns that arose as a result of his being appointed Bishop of Chichester and the large amount of work entailed in the administration of the bishopric, together with his very active interest in international affairs, found time to keep himself informed of activities at Tilmanstone Colliery. There had been a serious dispute at the pit which threatened the very good relations that had been built up during the time of Tilden Smith and there was a threat of strike action. However after some straight talking and some hard bargaining an agreement was at last reached. In May 1931, father received a letter sent from his home in Chichester from which I quote,

"My dear Mr Newman, As you know I have been deeply interested in events at Tilmanstone recently. It was therefore with much hopefulness that I read the announcement of a settlement in today's 'Times'. I do trust all is well. It must have been a very anxious time, and it will be a relief to be sure that all is rightly settled. Remembrance to you all, and to Mr Evans.

Yours sincerely,
George Cicestr.

Chapter 37

Brigadier General Sir Wyndham Deedes.
My stay at Oxford House, Bethnal Green January 1945.

It was January 1945 when my curiosity was further aroused concerning another character who my father seemed to know quite well. They were, by their position in life, their background and social standing, most unlikely bedfellows. My father, the working miner, union leader and left wing politician; the other a retired brigadier general, former Chief Secretary to the High-Commissioner of Palestine and later Malta, and member of a well-established family in Hythe.

It so happened that I was in my final year at Dover Grammar School for Boys, aged 17. That January, 1945, a Conference in World Citizenship was due to take place in Central Hall, Westminster and we had received notices at school of the event. I managed to obtain a ticket to attend the event which was to take place over a week, the problem was where to stay.

The War was still on and V2 rockets were exploding on London. I had a discussion with my father who was concerned as to the wisdom of going to London at this time. When he realised how deeply I felt and how keen I was to attend the conference, he said he would see what he could do about obtaining somewhere to stay during that week.

He went into what we called his office and took up the telephone. Mother and I were sitting having tea in the kitchen when he returned to join us. His first words were,

"Well, that's settled. You will have a place to stay for the week, so you make sure you behave yourself and take care wherever you go. The address I've been given is Oxford House, Mape Street, Bethnal Green. You will have to take a no.8 bus outside Charing Cross Station, which should get you there. Anyway you can always ask. When you arrive, preferably before lunchtime, you must report to the warden in charge, a Mr Roberts, and he will take care of you."

I thought that's quick and asked, "Who did you speak to?" He replied, "Wyndham Deedes, but you wouldn't know him. He lives in London and works for the government. He's an expert on the middle-east and I believe does some broadcasts for the government in Arabic. I doubt whether you will meet him." With that the conversation closed, but I was still curious and wondered what they had in common and how they had come to know one another so well.

A week later I found my way to Oxford House, met Mr Roberts and was introduced to other members of staff and shown to a room that was used as an office most of the time. A camp bed was brought in and made up. That was where I was to sleep.

Late that evening I had just got into bed when there was a loud bang, the building shook, the explosion did not seem very far away. I heard some rushing in the corridors and a young lady burst into the room and said, "Come on, we are all in the other room having a cup of coffee. We always get together when we hear explosions. It's a way of keeping up the morale." Suddenly an African student rushed in from the streets. They were all anxious to know what he was doing. Why hadn't he stayed in the safety of the underground? His reply was, "If I'm going to die, I'd rather die with my friends!" which brought forth both laughter and sympathy. The next day seated on the top deck of a bus travelling across London to Central Hall,

Westminster, we passed some streets where houses had been demolished by the rockets that landed that night. Smoke was still rising from the ruins.

The people addressing the Conference included the young fiery Barbara Castle, member of the Labour Party, Jan Masaryk one time Foreign Minister of Czechoslovakia, and leading personalities of the Conservative, Labour and Liberal Parties. It was an impressive occasion and the stay at Oxford House a great experience with such an intellectual and enthusiastic group of people.

Much to my surprise some years later reading Bill Deedes's auto-biography I found that he too, at a much earlier time, in the 1930s, had been put up by his uncle Sir Wyndham at Oxford House. It was at a time when his uncle was arranging for him to have interviews for a position as a journalist. Many years later Bill Deedes became editor of the Daily Telegraph and a minister in Mrs Thatcher's government.

It was later that I learned also of the relationship of Sir Wyndham and my father. It was still something of a mystery to me. I was reading through some of my father's letters when I read of a suggested meeting, proposed by Sir Wyndham, relating to the funding of the Elvington Settlement. Though I knew a great deal about the early Settlement and those associated with it I had never heard Sir Wyndham's name mentioned. But here it was in a letter to my father, the year 1939, just before the outbreak of war. He proposed that they meet together soon in order to discuss the funding of the Elvington Settlement. With the clouds of war on the horizon it would be necessary to allocate any moneys they possessed to those areas that might find themselves most affected by the war. Sir Wyndham wished to know my father's views on this most urgent matter.

As a youngster, I was well acquainted with many of the people who had worked at the Settlement. A flat was provided for their use. The various wardens during that period between 1925 into the 30s would visit our home to talk with my father.

They would often stay for a meal and became friends of the family. All of them made important contributions to the quality of life of the mining community and later in different ways to communities in different parts of the world. Miss Murray became well known for her work with refugee organisations people fleeing Nazi Germany. Miss Phyllian, an active member of the Labour Party, devoted a great deal of time on researching the work of "The Mechanics Institute". She later, as Dr Mabel Tylecote, became Lord Mayor of Manchester. Working at the University of Manchester, she spent a great of deal of energy working for better facilities for students and it is a tribute to her conviction, energy and work that many more young people were provided with the opportunity to study. In recognition of her work, one of the main buildings of the Manchester University has been named after her, "The Tylecote Building".

I later discovered that it was at the instigation of Sir Wyndham that these wardens were employed at the Elvington Settlement. Father had known him for a long time prior to their meeting in 1939, and that much of the success of the Elvington Settlement was down to the work of Sir Wyndham.

I was still puzzled by both his friendship with my father and his attitude toward the social and industrial problems. The description given by his nephew, Bill Deedes, of Sir Wyndham's association with the wealthy, among them the press barons, and how he organised shoots on his estate for these wealthy people, was very much at odds with the sort of person who would be a friend of my father. Then there was the fact of his army service at Gallipoli, and later his services as Chief-Secretary to the High-Commissioner of Palestine. This with his rank as a brigadier general and the fact that he had a knighthood, all pointed to him being very much a member of the Establishment, this at a time when the class boundaries were rigid and very difficult to cross.

It was purely by chance that I picked up a book from my father's collection entitled, "Out of the Pit". It was written by

John Newsom and published in 1936. He wrote in this book that "It was a challenge to the comfortable!" and dedicated it to Sir Wyndham Deedes. "I have no doubt," he wrote of Sir Wyndham, "that you will be, in private, this book's most severe critic and I offer it to you conscious that such a dubious honour will not affect your sound judgement. It ends where your ideas on such matters begin.

"I know that you will not rest until the note is sounded at whose behest all men of goodwill can rally to the construction of an England which will be comparable to the City of God rather than to the City of Destruction."

This view of Sir Wyndham was totally at odds with the one I had previously held which I had gained from his personal demeanour, which was of a rather unfeeling administrator. But my impressions were based on very brief instances and his position in society. A question of class prejudice on my part perhaps! To confirm the fact that I had been wrong, that he had indeed been interested in social problems, and of his practical engagement in such matters, was when I discovered, not so very long ago, 1960, a leaflet in my son's flat in Poplar, in the East End of London, which reminded young people that there was still time to apply for the "Wyndham Deedes' Education Scholarship."

This made me determined to look further into the activities of Sir Wyndham Deedes. Searching through the biography of Bishop Bell, I noted some references to Sir Wyndham; pages 135 and 291. Page 135 etitled, 'The Refugees' read:

"Hitler's advent to power in Germany in 1933 presented a portent hitherto unknown in modern European history. Nothing had been conceived on the scale and pattern of the Nazi resolution to purge the third Reich of all subjects of non-Aryan descent. The exodus of refugees began as early as April 1933.

"The problems of these Christians of mixed descent was first brought to the serious notice of George Bell by Sir Wyndham Deedes, who in August sent him a letter which he had received from Mrs Helen Bentwich, the Secretary of the German Refugees Hospitality Committee, pleading for action by the churches and by 'the complacent millions in England'.

"Again much later in 1945 relating to the matters of the Church in Germany, Guy Clutton Brock, religious affairs officer in the Education Department of the Allied Control Commission in Berlin, wrote to Sir Wyndham (19th August 1945), 'If you ever see the Bishop of Chichester, make him push the powers that be, to let him come out and see the confessional folk in Berlin. They are longing to see him.'"

These situations and their associations together over such a long period give some sense of the relationship that existed between Wyndham Deedes and Dr Bell, and their concern on these serious social matters.

I began to understand the relationship between Sir Wyndham and my father when I read these remarks made by Sir Wyndham on the establishment of the Settlement at Elvington in 1927.

He said, "It would be a good thing if people would only associate with each other in times of peace as they did during the war, and not have the class distinctions that are in force today. Industrial difference could be settled more easily if those concerned would meet to discuss them, as they would for a game of billiards etc. creating a community spirit, a spirit of co-operation, one with another."

Chapter 38

The Insurance Company. Miner's Compensation.

A great deal of time entailed in Billy's work as secretary of the Union was that spent on making claims for compensation to the insurance company employed by the colliery. These claims were made on the grounds of injuries suffered by men whilst working at the pit. This was by no means a straightforward process. Most of the claims made were rejected by the insurance company and often, to make them pay up, it was necessary to take the company to court and this was a risk.

The insurance companies could afford to employ top doctors and the best lawyers to represent them. It remained for Billy as union secretary to organise as best he could, with Mr Jack Elks, the regional official, a team of people who would best represent the claimants in court. This he did by getting to know members of the legal profession and doctors who might be sympathetic to the miners and their cause. Over time this is what he managed to do. Some became directly involved while others were always willing to give their expert advice. The lead member of the medical profession whom Billy relied on most was a Dr Ambrose Woodall, Head of Manor House Hospital. He and his associates would offer free advice and even provide representation in court if required. Though not always successful, they did win a number of cases.

However, there is a story that my father told me which has always stuck in my mind. It must be remembered that those representing the Colliery Company would provide opinions that contradicted everything the claimants said, interpreting any evidence in such a way as to appear that the claims made were false. Such claims would be dismissed by the courts and often the Union would have to pay the costs.

At one such hearing at which Billy was in attendance at the Law Courts in London, he was waiting by a phone booth intending to phone home. The door of the phone booth was slightly ajar. Billy recognised the person in the phone booth as one of the insurance representatives. His curiosity aroused, he listened and heard the man say, "Take on this man, we've won the case but arrange for him to be pensioned off within the month so that if anything were to happen you could not be held liable!" Billy moved away, found another phone booth, and phoned home to tell his wife what time he would be arriving home.

Those words of the insurance agent became embedded in his mind! "What action could he take? What action should he take, if any?" Then he remembered that there was a worker, an underground worker, who was well known for complaining of aches and pains which he said were due to his work in the pit. Up to now he had not been taken seriously. Even his friends didn't believe him. Billy, after much consideration, thought that it might be worth a try to make a claim on his behalf and if necessary take it through the courts.

Billy got in touch with his friends in London and asked them whether they could arrange representation on the Union's behalf in court. Billy told them that the weakness in presenting the case was whether the claimant was convinced enough of his situation to withstand tough cross examination in court. Was it possible to do anything about this?

They were invited to Manor House Hospital to meet the doctors who said they would see what could be done.

Billy explained to the worker that they were taking his case seriously but he would be required to undergo a thorough medical examination. And so it was arranged. Billy went with him to see the doctors in London. The claimant went in for examination and it was sometime before he came out. When at last he did come out his first words to my father were, "Billy, I may have felt bad before I went in for that examination, but believe you me, I feel a lot worse now! I wouldn't want to go through that again!"

The insurance company took them to court and much to their surprise lost the case. The Union's advisers told them to accept the award though it was less than they had claimed. Their advice was that if they challenged the amount awarded, the company would appeal and there was every possibility they might win the appeal and the claimant would lose everything.

The case was settled and the award accepted. The insurance company had to pay up.

Billy caught the train home, arriving in the evening. On arriving home his wife said there had been a telephone message from the agent of the insurance company who would appreciate it if Mr Newman would meet him at Tilmanstone Colliery next day. He left his number and invited Billy to ring back with a reply. A meeting was arranged away from the office, on a strictly one to one basis. Mr Newman insisted that there were to be no advisors or witnesses. The next day they met outside the pit gate and went for a stroll around the pit-top. After expressing their goodwill to one another, they soon got down to stating the core of the matter that had brought them together.

Mr Newman could see that the Insurance Agent was very concerned. It was he who had instigated the meeting and it is doubtful whether he would have done so without some instruction by the Colliery Company. "Now what is this all about? How can I help You?"

The Insurance Agent on the attack, replied immediately with the words, "Look Mr Newman we've met a number of times in attempts to settle claims of compensation brought by you or your union. Now look Mr Newman, you know as well as I do, that this latest claim had no substance, it was invalid and should not have been brought, and you know it."

Mr Newman: "Are you accusing the judge of bias? Are you willing to appeal and repeat those comments in open court? Are you questioning my integrity?"

The Agent: "I am suggesting that you and your advisors presented the case extremely well, but that the decision of the court was based more on its emotive content and the manner in which the claimant presented his case rather than of anything substantive. It was on the benefit of doubt that the decision was based. It was only on the basis that the amount of money involved in the claim was so low that we have not taken the judgement to appeal. But, come on, you know this isn't right! I didn't think this was the way you operated!"

Mr Newman: "Well, it maybe I have learned a few lessons from you and your associates. You or your company never cease to do anything but denigrate the claims that we put forward or to question the integrity and undermine the confidence of the claimant which often affects them so deeply that they not only lose their claim but detrimentally affects their whole personality. Many of these people, you know as well as I do, are thoroughly genuine and the injuries which they have suffered very severe. This kind of conduct I will not accept and whatever the consequences I will fight you. I can assure you, there are many more cases I can bring similar to the one under discussion, that is all I have to add. Thank you for the meeting."

The Agent: "Is there no way we can discuss this case, and the general situation that exists? The outcome of pursuing such confrontational policies does not benefit either of us, the Union or the company! If we could continue to talk for a little longer, What might you consider a reasonable basis for some prospect of negotiating any settlements?"

Mr Newman: "I might consider a situation in which only those cases that are not explicitly covered by the Compensation Act are brought before the court. All those that we feel genuine we try to settle between us out of court, and this for a trial period."

The Agent: "I will of course have to consult my company, but I'm sure that such an arrangement would meet with their agreement. Can we shake hands and hope it will prove beneficial to all concerned,"

And so began a long period of a mutual and successful partnership. They shook hands and parted.

Chapter 39

Tilden's Legacy.

The successes gained during the time that Tilden Smith was the owner of Tilmanstone Colliery, and the procedures of negotiation established, became so firmly embedded in the organisation that they lasted long after the unfortunate death of Tilden in 1930. Many of the facilities provided then are still in existence to the benefit of the whole community. The respect in which he was held by all who had anything to do with him is expressed in a letter to my father from George Bell, then Bishop of Chichester, agreeing with the words of my father, that "Had he lived he might indeed have shown the world how to solve the problem of industrial peace."

Chapter 40

Upbringing and Class Background.

During this time some notable personalities had been brought together by the enormous and severe social and industrial problems that were rife throughout the country and deeply affected Tilmanstone Colliery. The many personal associations and friendships made were kept up. They became enduring and lifelong. I still found it difficult to associate my father from such a humble background being accepted as a friend and equal to persons of such high social status. The social divide was firm and rigid. My father was brought up in the age when men of his generation were known as "doff capers" and old habits were hard to break. This made me intent on looking further into the backgrounds of these men.

They were all men who had lived through the tumultuous and tragic times of the First World War. Tilden Smith lost his only son, a dispatch rider caught in a gas attack on the Western Front. Tilden rarely spoke about it. Then there was Brigadier

Sir Wyndham Deedes who had fought at Gallipoli seeing all the tragic consequences of so many young men being killed on the beaches as they fought to establish a bridgehead. There was no place to hide. Then the difficulties of administration, and the suffering caused by the civil unrest during the occupation of Palestine where he served in Jerusalem as Chief Secretary to the High Commissioner.

I thought of Sir Wyndham as very much a member of the upper class, after all, the school he attended as a boy was the famous and prestigious school of Eton.

This attitude on my part was confirmed when I read, "The Problem of the Distressed Areas," by Wal Hannington 1937, published by Victor Gollancz Ltd, in which he tells how the voluntary organisation "The National Council of Social Services was taken under the wing of the government."

The desire of the government for the co-ordination of the various charitable schemes amongst the unemployed reached its culmination with the arrival of the hunger marches in London; as the Ministry of Labour report says, "The government accordingly decided in November 1932 (just after the big battles around Westminster) to recognise the National Council of Social Service as the appropriate central body for co-ordinating and stimulating schemes which involved the establishment of workcamps for the unemployed, where the conditions to say the least were very harsh. Any doubts about whether the National Council of Social Service was a purely philanthropic organisation, acting on its own, were well removed by the statement in the 1933 annual report of the Ministry of Labour which read: "The activities of voluntary organisations on behalf of the unemployed developed considerably during the year under the auspices of the National Council of Social Service, which undertook - at the government's request - the work of co-ordinating and stimulating this movement."

Soon after the big scheme was launched, Sir Wyndham Deedes, who had been a member of the council when it was an entirely voluntary organisation became the vice-chairman of the organisation, in place of R. C. Norman, brother of Montagu Norman, Governor of the Bank of England.

Wal Hannington asserts that "we would search in vain for any evidence of these honoured gentlemen ever having associated themselves with the demand for the abolition of the mean's test and the restoration of the benefit cuts." It is not surprising, therefore, that their new-found interest in the "welfare" of the unemployed through social service centres should give rise to suspicions in the minds of the workers. The conditions in these centres, better described as camps, was anything but the good life! They were both harsh and demeaning. The work could be well described as forced labour. "The good life," said the National Council of Social Service, "can only be achieved in a modern community if the spirit of voluntary service can be developed and made more effective."

"Such a phrase may sound wonderful to a gathering in a Mayfair drawing room, but it has little meaning to men and women whose lives have been stricken by poverty and unhappiness because they have been denied the right to work and earn a living."

It was not until some time later that I read in the book by John Newsome, "Out of the Pit", that I learned in spite of his social status in terms of class background and the part he played as an officer in the National Council of Social Service that Sir Wyndham was very much concerned with working class issues.

The whole ethos of the attitude of men such as Sir Wyndham, is plainly stated in the preface of the book, by the then Archbishop of York, William Ebor.

Relating to the deep and widespread poverty of the times, he posed the question "How much longer are we going to let this sort of thing go on?" He ends with the call to all men, "Remedy is never impossible where there are men who care enough!"

And these men did!

It was not till many years later reading Sir Wyndhams' nephews' book,

"Dear Bill, (1998, quote page 351) It may well have been that during this trip I felt, without being fully aware of it, a twitch on the thread. My uncle, Brigadier Sir Wyndham Deedes, after distinguished military service before, during and after the First World War, had decided while still a relatively young man to turn from public life towards the poor of Bethnal Green, and later to do what he could, for persecuted Jews of Germany. I had resided with him at Oxford House in Bethnal Green, during the years 1931-1939, without feeling, I have to say, the slightest compulsion to join him in his good works. But his example may have lingered in the blood."

It was thus that my doubts about the relationship between my father, Billy Newman, the miner and Sir Wyndham Deedes, the brigadier, were removed and I became convinced that there was a genuine friendship between these two men in spite of the great social divide.

The class difference was still exhibited in their manner of address. Sir Wyndham would often open a conversation with, "Newman, what can I do for you?" Father would then slip into his working class manner as speaking to a superior by saying, "Well, Sir! It's like this!" However this form of deferential attitude was soon forgotten since they both had a similar direction of interest. They had a common purpose.

The second person I mention, I have already referred to, was George Bell. He had a more direct influence on my father and perhaps on the social life of the people of the mining villages, particularly Elvington. He was, at the time, Dean of Canterbury and later became Bishop of Chichester. He and my father formed a close friendship which lasted a lifetime.

My father described George Bell as one of the most impressive men he had the good fortune to meet. Whether at Canterbury or Chichester his door was always open. There was always a warm welcome from Henrietta and himself over a cup of tea.

Amongst this galaxy of talented people who touched upon my father's life during this period was Dr Ambrose Woodhall, who was instrumental in founding Manor House Hospital, and served it as Chief Executive, and in his capacity as a surgeon for the greater part of his life.

He had seen much of the terrible suffering and many of the injured soldiers during the First World War. He was very grateful to Billy Newman for the great support he gave through the Miners Union to Manor House Hospital. They had many meetings during which time they became close friends.

Sir Ambrose Woodhall was not only instrumental in ensuring that miners and their families were given treatment in the hospital, but helped my father in a most active way in support of compensation claims made on behalf of the workmen. During the later years of his life, in recognition of his great public service, he was made a member of the House of Lords, Lord Uvedale. He never changed and always remained Doctor Woodhall to my father.

An acquaintance of my father through his contacts with Dr Bell, was R.H. Tawney. He knew little of his early background, but Billy kept himself well informed on matters relating to the Fabian Society, and the machinations of the Webb group. His name first came to my father's attention when he was appointed with Sydney Webb to sit on the Sankey Commission of Inquiry into the Coal Industry 1919. Largely due to the effort of Tawney and Sydney Webb the majority report came out with the recommendation that the coal-mining industry remain nationalised.

Father was presented with two of Tawney's books, one in 1920, 'The Acquisitive Society', which Richard Crossman, a Cambridge don and a minister in the 1945 Attlee government, described as his "Socialist Bible," and in 1931 a copy of Tawney's book 'Equality'. The writings in both books greatly confirmed my father's thinking.

However, it still remained unclear to me how people with such different backgrounds could at that time relate to each other. I repeat my father was a working miner, whose

education had been at a Board School, 1889-1897. He left school at 13, and since that age worked down the pit. Apart from the Board School, he was self-taught.

R. H. Tawney was born in Calcutta, India, the year 1883, to a family rich enough to enable him to attend Rugby Public School, and later Balliol College, Oxford. They lived in different worlds, divided by wealth and class.

None of father's class-mates achieved prominence enough to exert power. On the other hand, the same day that Tawney arrived at Rugby, William Temple registered at the school and they became firm friends. Years later William Temple became the Archbishop of Canterbury. Whilst a student at Balliol College, Oxford, another person whom Tawney made friends with was William Beveridge, who later was appointed Director of London School of Economics and after the War, during the Attlee government, became renowned for his production of the Beveridge Report, which was used as the foundation of the Welfare State.

Whatever their individual attitude was toward the working class, we rarely hear of working people being regarded as equals. In fact the majority of members of the working class did not regard themselves as equals. They looked upon those coming from the upper class, as experts, advisors, instructors or teachers, even within the WEA, as people who should be accorded the respect due to a superior class.

The barriers which prevented a breakdown of class division came as much from within the working class as from the upper class. The great difference was that the upper class possessed a degree of confidence in themselves that was lacking amongst members of the working class.

It was largely the effects on men serving together in the armed forces during both wars that many of the barriers of class division were broken down. The men fighting on the battlefields, regardless of rank, were dependent on one another for their very survival. They were more concerned with "Who was watching their back?" than, "What class do you come from?"

How far these men were influenced by the traumatic events that touched their lives is difficult to assess. I let the facts speak for themselves. Tilden Smith lost his only son, killed on the Western Front in a gas attack. Sergeant R. H. Tawney was rescued after being left for dead for some 30 hours in no-man's land during the Battle of the Somme, and his friend Captain Day was killed. Dr George Bell lost his two brothers at the beginning of the war.

Wyndham Deedes became a brigadier general and saw a great deal of suffering when serving in Gallipoli and later in Palestine.

The structure of class division may have softened, but in some respects it remained as strong as ever. It appears to be an integral part of the economic system, part of the free market capitalist economy, where some accumulate capital and possessions and the wealth that go with them, and others who possess next to nothing. There are still the masters and servants.

Chapter 41

Turning towards Political Action 1930 --1945.
Unemployment and the Hunger Marches. The Mosley Memoranda 1931 second Labour government.

The years 1930 to 1939, were for my father, years of marked contrast. Locally, particularly at Tilmanstone Colliery, due largely to the work of Tilden Smith in conjunction with the representatives of the workforce, the years 1925 to 1930 were relatively peaceful. The turbulent years of struggle, marked by insecurity, social unrest, militancy and strikes, were things of the past at Tilmanstone Colliery, though at Bettshanger Colliery in East Kent the traditional militancy surfaced with a strike during the war lead by a group of dedicated communists. However, the relative period of industrial peace in the district was in marked contrast to the suffering and unrest that afflicted miners in many other parts of the country.

After the debacle of 1926 the executive of the National Union of Mineworkers when confronted with the might of the government found themselves weak with no credible policy to offer their members. Many union members turned more towards political action to ameliorate injustice. They devoted much of their time to building up the Labour Party or joining such left wing groups as the Communist Party. In other parts of the country, particularly in the North and in South Wales, there continued to be great suffering. The numbers of men unemployed in these areas was extreme. During the winter months of 1933-34, the distressed areas of South Wales, Cumberland, Durham, Northumberland and the West of Scotland were scenes of riotous working class demonstrations, and agitations against the government. The economic measures imposed by the government in October 1931, which involved for the unemployed a 10 per cent reduction in their unemployment benefit and the application of the means test, produced even more acute suffering.

The Hunger Marches.
National Hunger Marches were a regular feature of the 1930s. In 1931 two-thousand five hundred marchers from the Midlands got as far as Hyde Park, where they were held back by "police baton charges". Their petition was never delivered to Parliament.

Three years later the "National Hunger March" on London took place. It drew support from all over England and Wales. It made its way peaceably to Whitehall where Ramsey MacDonald, Prime Minister leading the National Government, a supposed Labour Leader, refused to meet his own people. However, it was the march to London in 1936 known as the "Jarrow Crusade", that is best remembered. It was made up of 200 marchers from Jarrow. They walked some 300 miles with the message, "Send Us Work." Ellen Wilkinson, MP, marched with them all the way, only to learn that Prime Minister Baldwin was "too busy" to receive their petition." These were public demonstrations directed at the government and only incidentally against the owners of property. This was political action rather than attempts at direct industrial confrontation of unions versus owners.

George Lansbury Goes to Prison.
In the London boroughs of Poplar and Stepney there was a great deal of support given to the unemployed by public representatives led by their council leader George Lansbury. They claimed that "work must be provided or full maintenance paid to all." This claim was rejected and because the councillors refused to carry out government policy 29 councillors and Aldermen were arrested and sent to prison. Some 15,000 people came out to demonstrate their support for the action that their councillors had taken.

Not only did the workers have to fight the powerful owners of property and the representatives of the capitalist system, the Conservative Party, but had to fight many of their own leaders in the Labour Party. In the words of J. H. Thomas, the Railway Union leader, it was feared that 'Poplarism' would undermine the Labour Party's prospects of ever forming "a government again".

In The Times, Ramsey MacDonald wrote, "It cannot be over emphasised that public doles, poplarism, strikes for increased wages, limitations of output, that these could clearly not be socialist and misstate the spirit and policy of the socialist movement." However in nearby Stepney, the moderate mayor, Major Attlee, was preparing for his council to follow Poplar's example and support Lansbury.

Major Clement Attlee was to become the future Labour Prime Minister leading the famous Labour government of 1945. Unemployment had become the chief cause of what was described as "abject poverty" suffered by so many. It was a problem that could only be dealt with by government and though this was increasingly recognised by active politicians and intellectuals, it was not accepted by those in power, including leading members of the Labour Party, who felt that it was no part of their responsibility.

Those in public office, at the time, were far too much concerned with power and public acclamation than with need, policies and principles.

Strange to say, there was only one minister in the second Labour government who favoured a direct attack on unemployment. He was none other than the now infamous Oswald Mosley.

The "Mosley Memorandum" of 1931 included three main assertions.

1. Unemployment could be reduced by a public works programme of the sort proposed by the Liberal Party
2. He advocated that the machinery of government be changed in a way which made possible direct ministerial intervention in the management of the economy.
3. The memorandum stated that this would need "a mobilisation of national resources on a larger scale than had yet been contemplated".

He was advocating a form of Keynesianism as employed by the corporate state.

The scheme was rejected by the Labour government lead by the Prime Minister, Ramsey MacDonald, who was supported by members of his Cabinet including Philip Snowden and the young Herbert Morrison. The policy of MacDonald was surprisingly supported by Margaret Bondfield, the first woman Cabinet minister in government. They believed in orthodox financial policy which involved cuts in public expenditure. In August 1931 the National Government, led by MacDonald, implemented this policy with severe cuts in the public services.

It was estimated that one million men, women and children were reduced to living in abject poverty. It was seen that the problem of unemployment could not be solved by traditional methods of trades union action. Local union leaders turned more and more to Labour and Socialist Parties to bring pressure to bear on the government to implement policies to deal with the scourge of unemployment.

George Lansbury, who in 1921 led the "Poplar Rates Rebellion", having become leader of the Labour Party visited a fete organised by the Tilmanstone Miners, at the Barn in Tilden Smith's grounds at Eythorne. In the photo he is seen in the grounds against the backdrop of the Barn, with my Father and Lord Northbourne.

Billy Newman, who had been the first chairman of the Dover Divisional Labour Party since its inception in 1920, with other union members, saw it as their prime task to increase active membership of the Labour Party. The strong feeling of many of the working class, enraged by the attitude of their own leaders and those in authority, lead to the local activists supporting the left wing of the party. The communist parties benefited with an increase in membership, their leaders believing that only a complete change in the structure of society would solve the current problems.

The names of the communist Willie Gallagher and the Labour activists Manny Shinwell and George Lansbury were bandied about in conversation with friends across the kitchen table. Each of these men, not only addressed meetings and spoke on the public platform, but took part in direct action. Both Emmanuel Shinwell and George Lansbury were at various times visitors to Elvington and Dover at the invitation of my father on behalf of the Miners Union. Manny Shinwell stayed with us at Sandwich Road, Eythorne in 1930, when he came to open the new Pit Head Baths at Chislet Colliery. Some of those present at the ceremony were Mr Twigger, Billy Newman...

Chapter 42

Discussions across the Kitchen Table.
The 1930s. Schneider Trophy 300 mph,
Larwood body-line Bowling, Graf-Zeppelin 1938,
Boxing - Joe Louis v Max Schmelling. Etc.

Born in 1927, much of what I remember of the 1930s comes mainly from conversations that my father had with the family and friends who visited the house. My brother Richard Newman was born in 1907, and was some twenty years older than myself. He would have been 23 in 1930 and very much concerned with the great events of the times. This was manifest often in the exchange of ideas, which sometimes developed into heated arguments across the kitchen table.

The radio, which we were fortunate enough to possess, was built by one of the electricians at the pit. It became a great source of information, disseminating both local and international news. Few people owned radios at this particular time. The newspapers were compulsory reading in our household. They included the left-wing Daily Herald and on Sunday, Reynolds News. On occasion we would buy a copy of the Manchester Guardian, and sometimes the Daily Worker.

The topics of the day that I would take note of included those of more popular interest. I remember well talk of Malcolm Campbell breaking the land speed record in his famous car Bluebird. He was the first man to achieve a speed of 300 miles per hour, and there was much excitement. Then there was much talk of trouble between England and Australia caused by the advent of "Body Line Bowling". The fast bowler, Harold Larwood, a Yorkshire miner achieved notoriety by his actions. International boxing received great public attention, particularly when at their second meeting Joe Louise defeated the German Max Smelling. This was a blow to Hitler's claim of Aryan superiority and talk of the master race.

Later we watched the many aeroplanes, mostly bi-planes, flying over Dover out across the channel on their way to France, all part of the England to Australia air race. I was fascinated by the talk of the Schneider Trophy race which ended with England winning three times outright with speeds of over 300 hundred miles an hour in the year 1931. On the same day the world three kilometre speed record was broken by Fl-Lt Stainforth, at a speed of 408.8 mph.

These speeds were not matched again until the outbreak of war in 1939 by the Hurricane and Spitfire.

Fixed in my memory is the time, possibly 1938, whilst standing in the Elvington School play-ground, on a bright summer's day, and watching the enormous airship, the German

Graf Zeppelin, flying slowly overhead moving in the direction of Dover and the Channel. This was the first time we had seen such an aircraft and the last, and I just stood staring in disbelief. There was much talk, in the following year, of whether the craft had been sent on a military mission by the Germans to take photographs of our coastal defences.

Chapter 43

As a Young Child with the Biancies and the Gypsies.

As young children from the age of 5 years we would live in that wonderful world, filled with our dreams and vivid imagination. We tried to emulate our imaginary heroes. We became transformed. We took on many of those characters. One day it would be Robin Hood, another day Tarzan. I was always climbing trees or chasing across the large expanse of Waldershire Park, the Guildford Estate. As long as we were with friends our parents would let us roam freely. We were very lucky and very happy children.

Behind the Crown Public House in Eythorne there was a large field to which each year a fair would visit. In the middle of the field near a row of trees were situated two colourful, horse drawn caravans. These were semi-permanent.

One was occupied by the Biancies, and the other, a brightly painted gypsy caravan, by an elderly couple. The man I called Uncle Mark, and his wife I remember always colourfully dressed, in gypsy attire, as Aunt Annie.

Mr Frank Biancies' eldest son Roy and I would often meet together and play. Some Sunday mornings Roy would call round at the house and tell me that his father was taking out the horse and trap, and they were going for a ride round the country arriving back well before dinner, would I like to go? The three of us sat comfortably in the pony and trap on a beautiful sunny morning, listening to the clip-clop, clip-clop as the pony trotted along the tree lined roads of the countryside until we arrived at the public house, then known as "The Half Way House", on the Canterbury Road. There we would stop in the shade, and water was provided for the horse, after which Mr Biancie would buy a pint of beer, have a chat with the innkeeper and some friends, whilst we sat out in the sun enjoying a glass of orange drink. After about half an hour, we would be off again through the narrow lanes of Snowdown, Barfrestone and back to Eythorne, just in time for Sunday dinner. These were memorable times.

Chapter 44

Depression of the 30s' and the Silver Jubilee.

Through-out the 1930s there continued to be a great deal of suffering in terms of poverty and mass unemployment. To make matters very much worse there occurred the great Financial Crisis of 1931. Many firms went bankrupt. Financial institutions lay in ruins. National currencies became worthless, particularly in Germany. This was the time of Hitler's rise to power.

Strikes broke out in various parts of the country. Political action took place and public demonstrations were organised in support of the unemployed. There were the "National Hunger Marches" of the 1930s, and the Jarrow Crusade, with its plea, "Send Us Work".

For many of those suffering severe hardship a sense of hopelessness clouded the times. They felt left alone, isolated.

In the more prosperous parts of the country such problems receded into the background. Other more exciting events were at the forefront of the public mind.

Many people were dazzled by the great and spectacular events of the times. That which occupied the greatest public space was the Silver Jubilee celebrating the 25 year reign of King George V.

Many impressive functions were organised by the Royal Household. The press took it up. It became a prime matter of conversation by the public. Fetes, carnivals and parties took place in most of the towns and villages. The months of preparation with all its colour, pomp and pageantry engendered a feeling of excitement and wellbeing. Good cheer pervaded the atmosphere; eyes sparkling, children laughing, gathered in groups to go out to the fete and join in the celebrations. Forgotten were the unemployed. Forgotten were those who suffered.

A grand fete was held in the Elvington Sports Ground with exhibitions, football matches, sports and family races, food and ice-cream stalls and fun. To start the celebration in Eythorne a large number of villagers gathered together in the school playground, dressed in all sorts of fancy-dress, ready to take part in the parade along Sandwich Road, down Chapel Hill to the Elvington Sports Ground.

I well remember my friend Babette Latcham, 7 years of age, dressed as a cowboy astride a pie-bald horse, riding passed as part of the carnival and Police Constable Barham, with police helmet, white shirt and braces, suspenders and boots, shiny black boots, but no trousers. He bowed politely to all the ladies as he passed who returned his unexpected gesture with smiles of some astonishment. It was a great carnival and many of us followed behind to join in the parties at the sports ground where the people of Eythorne joined with the people of Elvington in great celebration. It was a bright sunny day full of excitement and fun.

Chapter 45

Troubles on the International Stage.
Helene G. C. Kuo, a guest.

Though the family joined in the celebrations, much of the conversation in our household was concerned with the more serious problems that were looming on the political horizon. A great deal was happening on the international stage. Hitler's army had marched into the Rhineland and the powerful German industrial complex was directed toward re-armament, the re-building of a most threatening war-machine.

In Germany coups were carried on at Hitler's behest, against some of his own henchmen. There was the night of the "long knives" when Dolfuss, a leading Nazi, was murdered on Hitler's orders. Concentration camps were being built, in which all manner of people were imprisoned without trial. Anyone, including many Trade Union representatives who were perceived to be a threat to Hitler's position of power, disappeared and were never heard of again. Rosa Luxembourg and the Socialist and left wing parties were destroyed. Campaigns were carried out against the Jews. Their shops were smashed and many were taken away and imprisoned. The Gypsies were hounded and treated as sub-human, unworthy of living.

"A sense of evil filled the notion of German Nationalism."

Many people in this country closed their ears to such talk. Many in government did not appear to take such matters seriously and simply ignored them. In fact some in high office treated Hitler and his henchmen sympathetically, regarding them as a protection against the spread of Soviet Communism.

It was the same with China, which was being attacked by Japan. Blood curdling stories were being told of the killings, rape and torture of many of the Chinese citizens. Such stories were not always seen in the regular press but were told by left-wing journalists and written of in books published by Victor

Gollancz as part of 'The Left Wing Book Club'. People in the towns of China were gathered together and the places where they were held were set on fire burning the people alive; men, women and children. Whole families were herded together and massacred. There are in existence written documents telling of such acts carried out during the invasion of Manchuria and in China with the infamous 'Rape of Nanking'. But these countries were a long way away, too far away to be of great public concern!

Nearer home in the latter 1930s, the Spanish Civil war broke out with the invasion by Franco and his armies from North Africa, supported by Hitler's and Mussolini's air forces, in a bombing campaign on open undefended cities. The 'International Brigade' was formed, consisting of volunteers to fight Franco. People came from many nations including France, America and Britain. Jack Jones, a trade unionist well known as a national leader; George Orwell, journalist and author of 'Animal Farm'; the famous American writer, Ernest Hemmingway and the well-known French writer, Andre Malraux were among those associated with the International Brigade. Tragically two miners known by many at Tilmanstone Pit lost their lives during the fighting. Their names were remembered, printed on a notice board in the miners' canteen.

Two events of the time stand out in my mind which make these memories so vivid. The first was when I answered a knock on the front door. It was about tea time on a beautiful summer's evening when three large men in camouflage battle dress stood at the door and asked to see my father. They were invited in and mother provided them with a meal and made them some tea. Their purpose was to raise funds for a new ambulance for their work with the International Brigade. They had come back from Spain, their mission was to replace their present ambulance that had been shot up, and stock it up with full medical supplies, before returning to Spain.

One of these warrior like men, dressed in military, camouflage uniform, seeing my curiosity, took me outside to show me the ambulance they had been driving. Inside photos of the many actions that they had been engaged in were placed around the sides of the vehicle. They showed men with injuries, buildings wrecked by bombing and enemy artillery fire, and pictures of refugees huddled together, seeking shelter from the hot sun, under the shade of the few trees. This incident more than any focused my young mind on the suffering caused by war, and the memory is still with me. They stayed with us a couple of nights before proceeding elsewhere raising further funds and equipment, and thereafter, returning to Spain.

Some months later whilst enjoying a late afternoon tea, after having been out playing, I answered a knock on the door, and was a little surprised at the sight with which I was confronted. I would have been eight years old. There before me stood a young Chinese lady dressed in all her finery. I had never seen a Chinese person before. I told her that my father wished her to "come in". I dutifully took her into the kitchen where the family were having tea. They all stood up and welcomed her with a shaking of hands. She was invited to join us and partake of some food and a cup of tea. We were all introduced. She spoke fluent English, and it was then I learned that she really had come from China and her name was Helina G.C. Kuo. She was very friendly and I was dying to ask what was that strange form of several metals rings round her neck? I was kindly, but firmly told by my father not to ask questions, so I just politely suggested that she might sign my autograph book.

I never did learn what the metal rings were for, or whether they indicated something specific. My presumption is that they were meant to be decorative, some sort of necklace, but I felt at the time that they must be jolly uncomfortable.

Helina Kuo it turned out was a Chinese government official who, with others, was touring the country to seek out people who would be sympathetic to their cause and bring to the attention of the world the cruelty being carried out on the Chinese people by the savagery of the Japanese troops. As regards actions which might be supportive of the Chinese cause she hoped that one might be the establishment of a "Boycott of all Japanese goods for sale in this country." She would be grateful if my father would introduce her to any local persons sympathetic to the cause and she was prepared to address any public meetings that might be organised to persuade the public of the urgency of the situation in China and seek their active support for her people back home.

Helina stayed with us for a few days addressing Union and public meetings and meeting a number of influential individuals who were prepared to help before returning to the Chinese Embassy in London. She wrote thanking mother for her generous hospitality, and my father for all his help. This was in December 1938.

Chapter 46

Settlement Wardens at Elvington. My First Days at Eythorne School.

Such events as meeting with and talking to these colourful personalities and hearing of their travels and adventures excited my imagination even at such an early age. I well remember the ladies who took part in welfare work among the mining community. They often came to our house, excited by the repartee and political conversation they would have with my father, and other guests, but perhaps more importantly because they enjoyed the cooking and particularly the bread made by my mother. I always remember Miss Phyllian standing, warming herself in front of the bright coal fire on a cold winter's day.

There was one special occasion which is stuck in my mind. It was when on one bright summer's day Miss Phyllian, wanting to leave my mother free to do her washing, drove up in her large grey open top car and took myself and some other children from the village out for a ride, ending up at St.

Margaret's Bay and the rocks. I felt very special riding in this big car with such an important person. It was a good day, and we laughed all the way.

But there had been less pleasant times that I well remember.

One such day was some years earlier when I was just four years old. I had just started at Eythorne Church School which was situated only two hundred yards along the road from where I lived. It was convenient for me and my parents. My brother Jackie, who was two years older, took me to school.

I had only been there a few weeks when we were told to line up in the hall. As we were lining up I heard a few whispers and noticed a man and a woman in white coats. The man was looking into the children's open mouths and prodding them with something. A sense of fear came over me.

Suddenly I broke ranks and ran hell for leather to escape. There was a hue and cry with teachers and pupils chasing after me. I ran into the cloakroom and dodged under the low bars, but eventually I was cornered and marched to Mr Southen, the headmaster, and given a smack across the backside and led straight to the dentist who inspected my teeth. This had been a traumatic experience, but worse was to come.

Some weeks later my friend Ruth Bowley turned up at the school. She asked to see me and wanted to know if I would like to go for a ride in her car. The year would have been 1931 and there were few cars to been seen. She said that Jackie could come along with me, for company, and so we went out and climbed in the car. I sat in the front seat. The car was a small Austin 7, brown in colour. We ended up at the Elvington Welfare Hall, climbed out of the car and walked to the door and then inside the building along a corridor. It was then that I saw the man and the lady in the white coats. I was seized by a dreadful premonition. I felt something dreadful was going to happen. I seized my opportunity, turned and ran as fast as my little legs would go! I went straight back to the car and hid behind it. I was driven back home where mother looked after me. She tried to convince me there was nothing to worry about and that it would have been for the best if I had stayed with the lady in the white coat. Mother told me she was called Nurse Nugent and she would have taken care of me.

Some days later, the lady, Ruth Bowley stood at the front of the class talking to the teacher. She went round the class talking to various children until she came and stood by me. She had a musical box with which I was allowed to play. I was asked if I liked the box and would I like to come for a ride?

I was taken by the hand, my mind taken up with the musical box, and led gently to the car. Before I knew where I was I found myself facing the lady in the white coat and being lead into a room with a large leather chair in which I duly sat, still playing with my musical box. It was magic! There was no man in the white coat who had so frightened me.

The lady in the white coat, Nurse Nugent, brought out some coloured balloons. She blew one up, a striking red one. She asked me if I would like to try and blow one up, and then another and I grew quite excited. The man in the white coat suddenly appeared and placed something over my nose and that is all I can remember. The next thing, I was back in the car with Ruth Bowley holding the musical box when I found that I had a number of teeth missing.

Ruth Bowley, a social worker whose office was at the Elvington Settlement, became a close friend of the family, a lady I will never forget.

Among the other social workers who spent time working among the families of the miners of Tilmanstone Pit, there are three others that I remember well. They include Miss Jan McDonald, Miss Mabel Phyllian and Miss Leake.

Miss Macdonald had worked as a librarian in Palestine and befriended many Arab citizens. She later retired due to ill health and lived for a number of years as a crofter in the wilds of Urquart near Elgin, in northern Scotland before moving in her later years to be near some of her Quaker friends, in the village of Chidiock, near Bridport in Dorset.

Miss MacDonald was a person of great intellect, with a

strong belief in social justice and possessing that precious character of deep determination, an amazing strength of will. In spite of her comparatively humble means she cultivated relationships with people of influence and power. She was acquainted with the likes of Brigadier General Sir Wyndham Deedes and Bishop George Bell and many associated with London School of Economics. She never hesitated to contact them if she required their help, and she inevitably received it.

Then there was Miss Phyllian, slightly more flamboyant, a graduate of Manchester University, who took on the role of warden at Elvington Settlement. She worked both among the families and studied the working conditions of the miners. I remember my father telling me how she persuaded him to take her down the pit to experience the real conditions under which the miners worked, where they were working in water and intense heat, and in places where they could hardly crawl. This would be in 1931 or 32. He insisted she dress up like a collier, hide her hair, and blacken herself up to look like a working miner. I remember we had a photo somewhere with her in mining outfit.

Miss Phyllian was an active member of the Labour Party. She returned home to Manchester and married a Dr Tylcoate. She worked at Manchester University and produced a detailed study of the Mechanics Institute and did a great deal of work for the Polytechnic which later became part of Manchester University, and bears her name, 'The Tylecoate Building.'

She became a Manchester City Councillor, and then Lord Mayor of Manchester. She thought a great deal of our family and for years afterwards when taking her holidays, visiting friends in Germany, she would stop in Dover and come out to Eythorne to renew old friendships and have a cup of tea. She had great respect for my father whom she regarded as an intellectual equal and often referred to him as a latter day "Socrates".

Miss Leake, I did not know so well, but my father held her in deep respect and she was a true friend. Brought up in a church household, her father was a cannon in the Church of England in Bristol. The family came to know her when she came to the Elvington Settlement as a social worker. She would visit our home to talk with my father and would fully enjoy the company of the family and friends.

I learned later that she had moved to South Africa, this during the 1930s, where she continued with her social work, working in a local, poorly staffed hospital. I still have a letter inviting my sister Violet, who had just qualified as a nurse, to come out and join her working in a native Hospital.

Miss Leake also founded a school in a country village for local African children. This I remember for when she came back on a visit to England, a car drew up and who came knocking at the door but Miss Leake. It would be in the 1950s. During the course of conversation father enquired where she was staying. At first she wouldn't tell him, thinking that father, a committed socialist, might not speak to her if he knew. However, she finally took the risk, and told father she was staying at Sandwich with her good friend Lady Nancy Astor.

Miss Leake realised that their political views were diametrically opposed, but hoped that this would make no difference to their friendship. Of course it didn't. Miss Leake continued and told dad that the school that she had set up and ran for the children, in the poorest part of South Africa, was funded largely through donations made by Lady Astor, and she came across to Sandwich every so often, to keep Lady Astor up to date with things in that part of the world. She stayed for tea before she returned to Sandwich, and later South Africa.

A few days later father received a card from Nancy Astor which read something to this effect, "Dear Newman, I've heard a great deal about you, the work you do and that you are an ardent Socialist. I would very much like to meet you and extend an invitation that you might visit and have tea with me at my house at Sandwich Bay. I am a great friend of Bernard Shaw, who too, is a great Socialist. Looking forward to an early reply. Nancy Astor." This was the last time I remember seeing Miss Leake, though we did receive the occasional letter.

Such were the people who during the time of Tilden Smith and afterwards in the 1930s did much at the Settlement giving their services to members of the mining community at Elvington and Eythorne.

Father continued with his work as Secretary of the Tilmanstone Miners Union, and worked to ensure the organisation was strong and efficient, and represented its members. There were a few incidents, expressing grievances which almost developed into unofficial strikes. Father always met the complainants on the spot. These incidents were soon dealt with on an amicable basis, both to the satisfaction of the men and the management.

Mr David Jenkins JP representing the management of the colliery as their director of finance wrote many years later that, "Billy Newman, as Secretary of Tilmanstone branch of Kent Mineworkers' Association, 1918 to 1946, and President of the Kent Mineworkers Association from 1921 to 1933, was instrumental in successfully negotiating the first wages agreement for Tilmanstone Colliery and later the first District wages agreement for the Combined Kent Coalfield. It speaks well of his leadership that whilst being instrumental in getting for the workers of the Tilmanstone Colliery the highest wages paid in the Kent Coalfield and thereby enabling the achievement of the highest output per man shift, only one day's stoppage, of a local nature, occurred through strike action from 1925 to 1946."

The relationships established in the years 1925-1930, between the Secretary of the Union, Billy Newman and the owner of the pit, Tilden Smith had been well founded, and proved long lasting.

Chapter 47

The Labour Party. 1935 General Election. Bennett v. Astor.

During the 1930s much of the talk in the house related to politics and the Labour Party. In the last parliamentary election held before war broke out in 1939, the Labour Party felt strong enough to put up a candidate to fight the local election. He was Mr Bill Bennett, the Chairman of Tilmanstone Branch. His opponent was Major J. Astor. Major Astor had represented Dover in Parliament as a Conservative and Unionist MP since 1922.

Billy Newman had a great following amongst the miners, particularly in Elvington and Aylesham. These were core Labour voters who would change the pattern of voting in the Dover District during the coming years. The problem, as always, was making sure that each and every one came out to vote. It was no use believing in the cause unless you registered your vote.

Billy Newman, along with many others in the Local Labour Party, worked hard in support of Bill Bennett, including key figures like Mr and Mrs Goodfellow, Sadie Coatsworth, and Mrs Brasier. One member of the party even volunteered to mortgage his house to cover any losses that might be incurred if the candidate lost his deposit. Such was the dedication and enthusiasm of the early members of the party.

I, myself, well remember the occasion. Some days before the election, I remember Major Astor visiting Elvington Council School. We were treated to a drink and cakes. Whether this was a deliberate political act or one of pure generosity, I do not know, but I do remember going home that afternoon and telling my father what a nice man Mr Astor was, and that he had even given us cakes, so we must vote for him. Father smiled, but nothing deflected him from his course. He would work and vote for Mr Bill Bennett. "You Tell Your Friends That!"

Major Astor the conservative candidate was again returned as the Member of Parliament for Dover with a substantial majority.

The Labour Party had now established itself as a powerful political force within the Dover District. A number of miners had settled in the surrounding villages of Eastry, Ashley, and Stonehall... and they supported the establishment of branches of the Dover District Labour Party within their communities. Local villagers joined the Labour Party including both farm workers and even some farmers.

Belief in the cause and optimism among the members gave great momentum to the recognition of the party and its principles. The participation of the WEA and the publications by Victor Gollancz of the Left Wing Book Club gave substance and information to the many thoughtful people in the party. The Miners Union contributed funds to the Dover Labour Party. The money went to pay for the hiring of halls and for the production of local pamphlets and news-sheets.

Members, like my father, knew they were on the road and must at some time be successful. They were men of principle. They had values and ideals and they knew how to organise and enthuse members of the public. They knew the appreciation people felt with a personal chat and a warm handshake.

At this time, an already well established organisation based on similar basic principles had developed in the Dover District. This was the Co-operative Society. After some years Billy Newman and a number of his friends were elected to the local board of management of the Dover Society, which had key properties in Dover town centre. Other premises were established on the outskirts of the town in Cherry Tree and Elms Vale.

The Co-operative store in River was the first that opened in the Dover District and was known as the "River and District Co-operative Society Ltd." It was well established having been founded in the 1880s by a Mr Radford.

In the 1930s, the period to which I am referring, the members of the committee of management included Mr R.

Sinclair, the President, Mr A.S. Haines, Managing Secretary, and Mr William Newman, Secretary of Tilmanstone Miners Union, was Vice-President of the committee.

I well remember the village store on Chapel Hill, Eythorne, the manager being a Mr Potts and his assistant Mr Clarke. The Co-operative store at Eythorne was just across the road from our house, and mother would often send me to the shop with her order book containing a list of groceries that she required for the week.

The Board of Management met regularly to check on the effectiveness of the organisation of the Dover Society and to discuss its policy. Quarterly meetings were held, which were open to all members, and progress reports were given at the meeting by the secretary and board members.

The Board of Management was elected by members at an annual meeting and was held accountable to members. Questions were put and resolutions moved.

These meetings were always well attended. The hall often packed with well over 100 members. Buses brought members from the mining villages of Elvington and Aylesham, adding to all those members living in Dover. These meetings were often very lively and many members from the floor contributed to wide-ranging discussions.

The Co-op in Dover was not just about its commercial considerations. On the social side it ran a long established library. I remember a Mrs Collins who lived in Glenfield Road, being the Head Librarian.

There were interests in education, and in the 1930s Sadie Coatsworth and Mrs Brasier had a great deal to do with the Co-op Women's Guild. They not only organised well supported social outings, bus excursions and parties, but were very much concerned with the political events of the day, and the ethos for which they stood. I remember my mother, often returning home from meetings of the Women's Guild, quoting the maxim, "Production for use and not for profit!" This was their cry! They were a force to be reckoned with, a growing influence on the left of the political divide in the Dover District.

They were beginning to be recognised as a challenge to the long established political parties in Dover. This expressed itself in the growing support and power manifest in the Local Labour Party.

Chapter 48

1939 County Council Election. Billy Newman Elected.

It was the year 1939, prior to the outbreak of the Second World War, that Billy Newman found himself standing for a position in local government. He was the Labour candidate for a seat on the Kent County Council representing the Eastry South Constituency, which included the mining villages of Elvington and Aylesham.

This candidature was none of his seeking. He had expressed no ambitions to seek political office. Billy's interest was primarily in serving the Miners' Union and in building up the Labour Party as a political force, not in seeking political office. However, he allowed his name to go forward.

It was no foregone conclusion that Labour would win. Billy fought to win but in his heart of hearts did not expect to be elected. The number of known Labour supporters in the area was, though substantial, still very much a minority. This area, which included many well established rural villages including St Margaret's, had up to this time been represented by Conservative candidates. The representative during this time had been Lord Northbourne. He was elevated to the Aldermanic Bench which created a vacancy on the County Council, and a Mr Rose of Sandwich had been selected to stand for the Conservative Party.

Mr Rose had a large general store in Sandwich, was well known in the villages and very much liked by his customers. It was presumed by the pundits that it was just a case of counting the votes and Mr Rose was bound to be elected.

How wrong can you be! An organisation seemed to spring into being from no-where, in support of Billy Newman. Co-op vans turned out carrying members enthusiastically shouting out their support. The cinema owner in Aylesham, Mr Chipper, offered the use of his car, and even provided the use of his cinema. There was no need to phone round and ask for volunteers. They were there in their dozens, all eager and ready to help. The miners and their families were solid in their support, and the children were singing, "Vote! Vote! Vote! For Mr Newman…"

The occasion was almost turning into a fete such were the lively and smiling faces. This was their occasion. This was their party! And they were the winners! Billy Newman topped the poll. He was the first Labour and working miner to become a Kent County Councillor. This was their triumph!

Chapter 49

The Rise of Nazism and the Drive against Russia.

The thoughts and political concerns of my father at this time were centred about the growing turmoil in Europe as expressed by the actions of Hitler and the Nazi Party and by the expansionist policy of Mussolini with his cruel ventures in Ethiopia. Then there was the Spanish Civil War with the Fascist destruction of a democratic government by Franco. The Nazis in Germany and the Fascists in Italy provided Franco with squadrons of war-planes to strike fear and horror into the population by flying low over undefended towns and villages to drop their high explosives, wrecking homes and killing whole families. This became a war of terror.

Latterly there occurred the Russian attack on Finland, a small sparsely populated country. The Finns fought bravely and aroused a great deal of public sympathy. But there were others who believed that the Finns were being used as sacrificial lambs and that the Russians were making a pre-emptive strike, to protect the security of their borders. Mr D.N. Pritt, a top lawyer and member of the Communist Party, gives an excellent account of this conflict.

For some years after the 1917 Russian Revolution and the seizure of power by Lenin and the Communist Party in Russia, the Western Powers including the ruling establishment in England, encouraged and supported the 'White Russians', in their military ventures to win back power.

Hitler's openly declared policy was the conquest of Eastern Europe, which included parts of Russia in order to gain "Lebensraum". In Germany the Communists and Socialist Parties had been growing in strength under the dynamic leaders such as Rosa Luxembourg. They were perceived as a threat to the established capitalist ruling class and industrial barons such as Thyssen and Krupps. Hitler and his Nazis took on the Communists using the most brutal methods, killing their leaders and sending Party members and sympathisers to Concentration Camps never to be heard of again. The Communist influence in Germany was eliminated.

Many of the influential leaders in Britain, government Ministers, newspaper Barons, the rich and powerful in society, regarded the Nazi activities against the Communists and left-wing leaders, with a great degree of satisfaction. Any aggressive intent that appeared to be directed toward the East and Russia, was applauded in the West.

And so it was among circles of the establishment that the building of strong fortifications on the Soviet frontiers was to be encouraged. With the help of the British, but more so the Germans, the Finns built a strong line of fortifications on the Soviet frontier known as the Mannerheim Line. Military tacticians perceived this as providing a jumping off ground for a possible attack on Russia. It provided a vantage point which would make the defence of Leningrad difficult if not impossible. It was suggested that this was a motive for the

Russian attack and the six months war, which resulted in Finland ceding the frontier zone to Russia.

These thoughts, these perceptions, were very much to the forefront of the strong discussions that took place between my brother Richard, now in his 30s, and my father, across the kitchen table. Both had visited Germany during the Hitler period. Both had made friends there, hearing the different points of view held by people with regard to the Hitler regime. Father kept contact with some of his Trade Union friends he had made on his 1930s visit to the coal mines of Essen, and on other occasions.

But suddenly all correspondence stopped. All communication ceased. We continued to learn a little of what was happening in Germany through our friend Bishop George Bell, who maintained close contact with some of the Church leaders in Germany, including Bonnehoffer, later executed by the Nazis.

The amazing fact was that our latest guest, Vera Gorkenant, a middle class university student from Berlin, her father a bank manager, kept contact with my sister Betty, even during the first week of the war. She even sent my sister a present, a pair of silk stockings, and the parcel got through. She was incidentally a member of the Hitler Youth, aged 18 or 19, but a quite thoughtful and pleasant young lady. Vera, enjoyed herself, meeting many of the local villagers, when she attended the dances held at the Barn. She could not believe there would be a war between our two countries. She stayed with us at our home in Eythorne in the year 1939, just two weeks before the invasion of Danzig, when she was ordered home by the German authorities. It was at the time of Hitler's threat to take over Danzig.

This was the deeply political atmosphere that I experienced during my childhood. The varied and rich personalities we met, all impressed themselves on my mind.

In 1938, aged 11, I was accepted as a student at Dover County School for Boys. That summer, I went with my sisters on holiday to Devon. We visited Plymouth and stood by Drake's statue on the cliff. We had a grand view of Plymouth Sound and the sea. There at anchor were two great naval vessels, the Ark Royal and the Courageous, both aircraft carriers. It was a sight to behold. Unfortunately they were both sunk early on in the war and many brave sailors were drowned.

Part 3

The War and its Aftermath

Chapter 50

And So War Came. 1939.

That summer father took my mother and Mrs Friar on holiday to Devon. When he heard that Hitler was threatening Danzig he came straight home. I remember it well. It was a beautiful hot summer's day and I was playing with Ernie Stock. We were climbing on the roof of our shed, enjoying the sun, when we saw a bus load of evacuees from the Chatham area, arriving at Eythorne School.

It was soon after father returned home that notices went out for us to go to Eythorne School and collect our gas masks. The government were preparing for any eventuality. There were radio news bulletins every hour.

That Sunday morning I attended Chapel. I was returning home, walking up Chapel Hill, when my father met me. He said that Germany had not replied to the ultimatum at 11 o'clock, and that we were now in a state of war with Germany. Almost immediately the air-raid siren sounded. We learned later it was a false alarm.

It may sound strange, but I was more concerned about our dog than anything else. We had a wonderful St Bernard dog. He had been with us since I was 6 years of age and it fell to me to take him out for walks most days. He became my friend, was a wonderful companion and I always felt safe with him. The immediate question I put to my father was, "What would we be able to do for him if there was a gas attack? He's too big for a gas-mask!" My father calmed my concerns. He assured me that he would be looked after. We would have towels ready to be soaked in water to put over his head. This would stop gas getting through and protect him. Such devices had been used by soldiers, with some success, during the First World War. Dad sounded very convincing, and so we went home to listen to the latest news on the radio and have our Sunday dinner.

Danzig was taken and soon afterwards Poland faced fierce attacks and was invaded by both Germany and Russia. France had joined with Great Britain in the fight against Hitler's regime in Germany.

During the early months not much action occurred on the Western Front. The Germans remained behind the Siegfried Line, while the Allied forces manned the Maginot Line. This period became known as the phoney war. The popular song of the time was, "We are going to hang out the washing on the Siegfried Line, have you any dirty washing Mother dear!"

In the East the Germans were attacking Poland with great ferocity, whilst in the West nothing much appeared to have changed. Life went on very much as usual.

Locally the villages such as Eythorne, where we lived, were soon to be greatly affected. Gone would be the calm, quiet, the customary routine of village life. There suddenly arose a buzz of excitement, as columns of military lorries blocked the lanes on their way to Waldershare Park. There, the lorries stopped and out climbed the soldiers. A strange looking lot they were!

They were not dressed in the uniforms that we had taken as normal for soldiers, but wore multi-coloured skirts, 'Kilts'. Needless to say, we soon learned that they were a Highland regiment, from Scotland, the famous 'Black Watch'. Tents were soon erected and the area of their encampment fenced off. These regular soldiers soon settled in, visiting the pubs and making friends in the village, and many catching the bus to Dover in search of further entertainment. In some cases, it was a question of "Lock up your Daughters".

A few weeks later another regiment came and formed an encampment in a neighbouring position in the park along the Coldred Road, near Canterbury Gate. This regiment, an infantry regiment, was a branch of the Royal Fusiliers.

These regiments were to form the first of those which sailed across to France to form what became known as "the British Expeditionary Force". Later other regiments such as the Somerset Light Infantry and the Queen's Westminsters took their place in Waldershire Park, before embarking for France. Bren-gun carriers, motor-cycles and side cars soon became a common site.

There was some nervousness relating to the possibility of a surprise invasion. One incident I remember well was within months of the beginning of the war, my friend Bobby Trice and myself out riding our bicycles saw some white dots high in the sky. It was a fine, warm, autumn day. The dots in the sky appeared to grow larger as they floated in the blue towards Elvington. We raced on our bikes in the direction that these parachutes were floating. When we passed through Elvington, we found the side lane leading to Knowlton lined with troops in motor cycles and side-cars demonstrating preparedness in case the parachutists should turn out to be German. We were turned back before we reached Knowlton and were told that one of the men was caught up in a tree and a soldier was on guard duty, waiting for an officer to arrive. It was learned that he was British and he and his crew had escaped from a Blenhein bomber which later crashed near Aylesham, returning home from northern France. We did not see many aeroplanes in those early days of the war.

At this time, all the regiments were infantry regiments, members of rifle brigades, and memories of meeting these soldiers in the village were very much brought to the forefront of my mind when the Battle of Calais was being commemorated some 50 years later.

Jean and I, as Mayor and Mayoress of Dover, had the privilege of being invited by the Colonel of the Regiment, General Sir Robert Pascoe to be among his guests.

We were entertained in the Captain's cabin by the captain of the cross channel ship, Captain Peter Hogg. Those present included Lt Colonel Palmer and his wife; the general in charge, Colonel of the Regiment General Sir Robert Pascoe; and the

Queen Mother's Equerry, Sir Martin Gilliat. They were all representing the Green Jackets, the infantry regiments that had fought so heroically in the Battle of Calais.

Before leaving harbour we went up onto the bridge and during a conversation I had with Sir Martin Gilliat, he told me how pleased he was to be a member of the party for he had been one of those young soldiers who fought in the Battle of Calais and how it brought back many memories, particularly of his friends who fought so bravely and gave their lives. Sir Martin himself was injured, a battle casualty, shot in the head. He said that when he regained consciousness he found himself in a German field hospital being treated by a friendly German doctor. He spent the rest of the war in a prisoner of war camp. There is a lot more to tell, but that is part of another story, my story.

Father's visit to Berlin.
My father did not believe that there could be peace with Hitler and the Nazi regime. They were destroying in Germany everything he had come to believe in. Here was a government which would not tolerate any form of dissent. This view was not based on left wing propaganda, it was based on personal observation. On his visit to Germany he had attended political meetings accompanied by his German friends. They told him to stick close to them and to keep quiet, complete silence and not to utter a word. If the crowd cheered or clapped he should behave in a like manner. It could be dangerous for them if they were seen to behave in any other way. There he saw and heard for himself the proclamations made by the party activists which were both dangerous and provocative. The behaviour of the crowd had to be seen to be believed. The manner in which the meetings were conducted, and emotions aroused gave a sense of a fearsome unity of thought and purpose.

"When the meeting ended and we were back on the street, we felt somehow more secure. We were back in the world of reality. The stars were still in the sky. A slight warm breeze cooled our cheeks. As we distanced ourselves from the meeting hall we began to relax, engage in measured conversation and look forward to a good night's sleep."

This was during the summer of 1936. Hitler had been in power just 3 years, and now in 1939 we were at war. During the early years of the time of the phoney-war, we, in the West, wondered when the storm would break; and it would break, for there was no room for compromise! And if the Nazis did succeed and this was very likely, father said he would be among the first to be taken. If we were to be victorious, it would be a long war.

In my father's view it would be a long time before we would see peace again and experience life in a settled world. As far as those about him were concerned, he showed little emotion, but always projected a calm, purposeful image. He knew what needed to be done. He had a clear sense of direction and articulated it with clarity.

Chapter 51

County Council and Local Constituency Work.

Billy Newman, besides his many other activities, was now on the Kent County Council representing Eastry South which included the mining areas of Aylesham and Elvington. Here he was able to gain information on a wider basis concerning plans that the County Council had, which might affect the Dover area and the miners in particular. There were important local issues to be dealt with involving the relations of the management of the colliery and the local council. Matters of particular concern included health and safety and working with the military regarding the use of facilities at the pit. Such an example was the use of the pit baths by the soldiers encamped in Waldershire Park.

A letter was received from Brigadier Sir Wyndham Deedes relating to the funding by the National Council of Social

Services to the mining community. Sir Wyndham was secretary of that organisation. He suggested in his letter that it was urgent that they should meet and discuss the situation. The outbreak of war would mean they would have to reassess on a national basis where any such funds they had should be directed. This meant that the funds that had been forthcoming over the years to the Settlement at Elvington would no longer be available. This was in the year 1939.

Billy met Sir Wyndham at his flat in London for lunch and discussed matters of mutual concern. There was a frank exchange of views by two friends both outspoken, putting their interests strongly, but equally, they recognised the realities of the situation. Because of the critical situation we were facing as a country, and the emergency services crying out for funding, it was decided that the funding directed to Tilmanstone would be stopped for the time being.

Sir Wyndham said that if any situation should arise where he might be of help, to contact him directly. He gave my father his personal telephone number. Sir Wyndham was a good friend to have. He would prove so useful in many ways. If he could not help you with a problem he often knew someone who could. And so it fell to the Union, the men themselves, and the directors of the pit to find any funds that were necessary to support the welfare and the Settlement.

The necessity of keeping the Union strong with a full membership was an urgent priority, both for the purpose of raising funds and more importantly for maintaining that sense of solidarity and purpose amongst the local community. Committee members helped the secretary in this work, but my mother did a great deal helping my father with the paper work. This involved checking the members paying-in books and the transfer of the figures to the balance sheet, checking and double checking them.

Regular union meetings continued to be held at the welfare hall. The organisation was both efficient, effective, and well supported. The management and union met together to consider the drastically changed situation that they were all facing. Conditions at work assumed a central place in their talks in terms both of 'Safety and Payment'. Regular meetings and social functions were held. The form and structure of the organisation itself assumed an even more central importance. It was necessary to engender that feeling of belongingness and solidarity, so necessary in keeping the men together.

Tilmanstone Colliery was plagued by the particular problem of water and if the pumping facilities were damaged severe flooding would occur in the pit. An explosion near the pumps would be critical for those working in the mine. The men were united in their call for safety precautions and military protection. The miners were very much aware of a possible attack and the dangers of bombing. A solitary anti-aircraft gun was eventually placed near the pit top. The first-aid building was enlarged with better equipment and more training provided for the staff.

One evening Dr Bellamy, the local doctor, came to see my father to talk over medical facilities available in the village. He said there was only his surgery available to the community. The question was, what if any emergency arose would be expected of him? He informed my father that he had been asking persons in authority if any land might be made available for building a local health centre for the village and could they point him in the direction of any such person, or group of persons, who might help in this respect.

He felt he was getting nowhere, when it was suggested by a prominent person that if anybody could get things moving, it might be Billy Newman and he would be well advised to go and see him! "So here I am! If there is anything you can do I would be grateful." Father said he couldn't promise anything, but since he completely agreed with everything that had been said, he would see what could be done.

Father contacted the management at the pit and the directors in London, Lord Northbourne and members of the Kent Health Authority and Sir Wyndham Deedes among others. He felt no door should remain unopened. There was much behind the scenes activity and finally Dr Bellamy phoned to say that they had been offered a plot of land and funding to build and equip a health centre as suggested. This was a great step forward and thanks were expressed to all involved.

Units of the Home Guard were formed and people were appointed as fire-watchers. Observation posts were established at various points. Mr Rice, believed to be a Nazi sympathiser and an associate of Oswald Mosley was moved out of the area under the 18b regulation. Observation by the authorities was directed to known Communists and their sympathisers. In fact soon after the out-break of war two Army officers called at the house, much to mother's consternation, especially when they asked for father. He was out, but they came back later when father returned and were invited in for a cup of tea.

Afterwards, I asked what that was all about? Father said they were trying to gain information about the local people, who might be subversive. They particularly questioned people like himself with left-wing views, the Communists, and surprisingly they questioned him relating to his meetings with Mr Rice. "The only information I gave them about people in the village, including Mr Rice, was that they behaved like perfectly good, patriotic citizens. However the Army officers did at one point press me on my knowledge of the young Mr Rice.

"I was however, surprised that they knew Mr Rice had visited me in our home a few times. The conversations between myself and Mr Rice covered the dangers inherent in the world situation, and we did talk of how they might affect matters in the local area with its rich assets of coal and the very productive areas of farmland. Mr Rice, like all of us, wondered what would happen if the worst occurred and the Nazis took over, but nothing specific was discussed. A sceptic might have thought that he was putting out feelers to find out whether we, the miners, would be prepared to discuss with him what arrangements might be made if there were a Nazi Occupation.

Nothing tangible was suggested. It did appear, from the knowledge these two officers possessed, that the telephone messages to the house had been intercepted."

In terms of domestic issues food rationing was imposed. Some miners had the foresight to alleviate such shortages as might exist by setting up a "Pig Club". Matthew Batey was in charge. He lived in Elvington. Those interested were asked to take out shares in the project. This enabled those organising the venture to raise enough money to buy the animals and the necessary equipment for the start-up. Some members volunteered to collect any suitable waste products for feeding purposes. The club proved a great success, providing during the course of the year food for a veritable feast for its members.

Farm workers and poachers became quite popular figures in the village. The farm workers were legally empowered with gun licences and the land owner's permission to shoot on the estate. The poachers took their chances with the law. Both would be welcomed by the housewives when they brought a rabbit or a pair of pigeons for the table. Most of the family food was bought at the local village shops. There were three medium size grocery shops in Eythorne, the Co-op, Vyes Stores and Rigdens.

The bus service from Dover, via Whitfield and Eythorne to Elvington was frequent and regular, and villagers took advantage of the bus to go to Dover both to visit the shops and for entertainment. The cinemas remained open, the Regent, the Plaza, the Kings Hall, and the Granada. They were always, if not full, well attended particularly at the weekend. Any dangers that might exist were simply ignored by our friends. The changed way of life, by the few who remained in Dover, was taken for granted, even later on in the war when such dangers included bombing, shelling and the menacing doodlebug.

Beneath the trees near Knowlton tanks were hidden. They would use the valley between Knowlton and Elvington as a tank training ground. In some fields hundreds of posts were set up to prevent the possible landing of enemy aircraft.

Defensive networks were built taking the form of dug-outs, and concrete bunkers, generally on the crest of the hills. On the Shepherdswell and Eythorne railway line, a large eight-inch artillery gun could be seen. Winston Churchill and his War Staff visited the Eythorne site, however they appeared more interested in a dog they encountered, a 'Great Dane', than in the gun they had come to inspect.

I remember the gun well. A group of us were waiting at the bus stop, on the corner of Sandwich Road, by Bradley's shop, the newsagents. There was a tremendous bang and a whiz as the shell passed overhead. Everybody instinctively ducked. Then Mr Bradley came running out of the door and started to close the wooden shutters on his windows when suddenly there was another enormous bang and in spite of all his efforts, Mr Bradley's windows were completely shattered. He looked like a man in utter despair. The bus came on time, with a cheery lady bus conductor and we were soon off to Dover.

For some time we had to possess a special pass to get into Dover. Check points had been set up at various places of entry, including near the bottom of Whitfield Hill.

As the war progressed, with the capture of France by the Germans, the experience of war for many of the civilian population became an almost daily occurrence. A new phase of warfare affecting this country was about to begin, that of total war.

The German military machine with all its might was now only 20 miles away. Airfields were built to house the fast, deadly Messersmitts and Junkers bombers ready to attack the English mainland. Well-equipped heavy motor-torpedo boats, the fast and effective E-Boats, were stationed close by in the channel ports of Calais and Boulogne. Mines were laid by both sides in the Straights of Dover to stop shipping using the Channel. Tragically, soon after the beginning of the war, a friend of the family who lived at Whitfield, Mr Hopkins, was drowned when his ship struck a mine. He was a pilot operating from Dover, guiding ships up the Channel.

Churchill visits
Channel guns

ONE of the most interesting photographs to come to light as a result of the recent exhibition of pictures of old Eythorne, put on by Mrs Sue McNeilly, is the view above of Britain's war premier Sir Winston Churchill outside the old East Kent Light Railway Station.

Mr Churchill, as he then was had arrived in East Kent to inspect some of the long-range guns sited in this area to counter the enemy's long-range shelling offensive. One of the railway mounted guns was located nearby.

Here, on September 12, 1940 Churchill, joined by Mr A. V. Alexander, First Lord of the Admiralty, Admiral Sir Dudley Pound, First Sea Lord, General Sir Alan Brook, Commander in Chief Home Forces and General Sir John Dill, Chief of the Imperial General Staff, is pictured taking time off to meet the local people.

Charlie Simpson, of Elvington, was chuffed when Churchill paused to pat his great dane but, sadly, his pet died unexpectedly the next day.

Owner of the photograph is Mr Bill Newman, of Beresford Road, River.

Early in the war, we could see several destroyers, part of the Dover Patrol, at anchor in Dover Harbour. The destroyers soon became a target for German bombers and suffered a great deal of damage and so it was found necessary to move the destroyers elsewhere. The Dover Patrol was disbanded, but the port remained a naval base to a flotilla of motor torpedo boats, including a Norwegian Section. They were used to lay mines in shipping lanes off the coast of France and make commando raids on the French coast.

Flying high over the harbour were the barrage balloons providing a defence against low flying enemy aircraft. I well remember cycling to school with my friend Peter Bean and arriving early at school. We were the first to arrive. It was 8.30 am and we stood in the playground, looking out over the harbour when to our complete astonishment we saw two planes come in low and shoot at several balloons which became immersed in smoke and gradually sank slowly to the ground. As quickly as they came, the planes had turned and gone. They had flown in, low, under the radar and had achieved complete surprise. This was repeated several times during that week.

School continued much as usual though we had a number of practice moves to the air-raid shelters which had been dug into the chalk face the other side of the school hall. The only real exception was in the change of timetable to facilitate the establishment of a vegetable patch to provide food and help with the war effort. This was supervised by Mr Teddy Archer. This venture was just coming to fruition when it had to be left to its own devices. We left the school. We were evacuated.

In June 1940 with Germans on the cliffs at Calais, and with invasion expected at any moment, the schools in Dover were told to evacuate. Parents received a letter from the Headmaster, Mr J.C. Booth, MA (Oxon.), outlining the procedures to be followed at Dover County School for Boys. It was a bright sunny June morning as we arrived at the school between 8 and 8.30 am in June 1940. We lined up on the bottom playing field and were told to be with a friend. My companion was Ken

Norton and we stood together ready to march off with our form teacher down Folkestone Road to Priory Station. There we boarded the train in a section that had been reserved for us, while other schools, including the County School for Girls, did likewise. Most of us had a small case or a satchel which contained the bare minimum of essentials, a bag with sandwiches and a container, (non-glass) for drink. It was a hot June day. We didn't know how long we would be on the train. All we knew was that we were going to South Wales. It was a long hot day and it was not until 5 o'clock that we arrived in Ebbw Vale where the school would remain for the next four years. Incidentally, I did return home to Eythorne for some of the school holidays, and experienced much of what was happening, due to the war, in Dover and the surrounding district.

Father continued work as usual down the pit. He received time off when necessary to attend County Council meetings at County Hall in Maidstone, many of which were concerned with the ramifications of the war effort. The only vehicles on the road during these times were military vehicles heading toward Dover. Maidstone was some 40 miles distant and the round trip meant a journey of some 80 miles. He was given a special petrol ration to engage in his County Council duties. We had a little old Austin Seven car and needless to say the journey was slow and took some time.

Some six months after the schools evacuation to Ebbw Vale, a town at the head of the valleys, dominated by the steel works and coal mines, the Kent County Education Committee responsible for the school sent County representatives to observe the facilities available for the children.

When the Headmaster, Mr J. C. Booth, came into our classroom it was much to my surprise to see that the County Education Officer was accompanied by none other than my father. He got in touch with me later that evening.

Some months later I received a brief letter from my father informing me that the County Council were taking part in the "Evacuation Scheme" to send children to America and other far off countries in the Commonwealth for the duration of the war. His question was would I like to go, and if so to fill in the form naming the countries in order of preference and send it back by return of post. He gave no advice, apart from saying it was my choice, feel free! For a moment I felt completely alone. I was filled with doubt and indecision. It meant crossing the Atlantic with the possibility of being attacked by German U-Boats. There was nobody to help. It was for me to decide.

Considering the opportunity being placed before me I studied the letter with great care over breakfast, before going to school. I came to a decision and signed the document to the affirmative, sealed the stamped envelope and put it in the post-box at the end of the road. A few days later I had a medical and everything was set up to depart for embarkation when the tragic news hit the headlines, "The Sinking of the St Benares" with the children on board. The Evacuation Scheme was immediately stopped. I stayed with the school in Ebbw Vale for the next four years.

Billy Newman was very much a man of the local community. He was always out and about around the village with the people. He was at his busiest with Union business which as far as possible he integrated with the work he did with the Labour Party and Co-operative Movement.

Chapter 52

1945. The End of the War in Europe The Election.

At the end of the war the great election of 1945 took place. Elections had been suspended for the duration of the war. The last election had been held in 1939, and Mr Churchill's government had been in office continuously since 1940. For some years there had been talk about what was to happen when peace reigned once more. What kind of country would the soldiers, sailors and airmen returning from the battlefields want, expect and deserve? As early as April 22nd 1944 my

Father took me to Canterbury Cathedral to listen to Sir William Beveridge speak on his plans for "Social Security", the forerunner of the Welfare State. The Archbishop of Canterbury was in the Chair. The Plan outlined by Beveridge formed the basis of the legislation enacted by the 1945 post-war Labour government.

There were some strong personalities in the Labour Party, such as John Stratchey, Stafford Cripps, Hugh Dalton, Ernie Bevin, Herbert Morrison, Aneurin Bevan, the young Harold Wilson, Harold Laski and of course the seemingly unassuming leader of the party, Clement Attlee. Though there was general agreement in principle on Socialist objectives, there was a great deal of difference of opinion about how such objectives should be reached. Some leaned very much to the left while others were very right wing. There was a great deal of dissension, often expressed in public, between various members of the party. Near the start of the general election campaign there were attempts by Herbert Morrison and Harold Laski to depose the current leader of the party, Clement Attlee. Ernie Bevin, a loyal supporter of Attlee, when he heard of it immediately acted to stop any such move and expressed in no uncertain terms his opposition to a schemer such as Morrison.

When the election campaign started the Labour leadership were united, but while there was hope there was no anticipation that Labour would win, in spite of the fact that Attlee had been Deputy Prime Minister to Churchill throughout the war. It was Churchill who was the publicly acclaimed War leader. He was the hero of the nation. Victory had been achieved and there were widespread feelings of thanksgiving and vast celebrations were held on the streets of every village and town.

It was obvious that Churchill, the war hero would be re-elected. It could not be otherwise. Attlee was a quiet man, and he was no orator. Churchill knew how to use the radio, a colourful character and a most impressive public speaker. Everything was seemingly in his favour. The question was, would he do as much for the people of this country in time of peace as he had been able to do during the war. He had brought victory, now could he provide the kind of country that those men fighting at the front, whether in the air, on the land or at sea, the kind of country in which they wished to live, and felt they deserved to live.

As the results started to be announced on the radio that evening there was an atmosphere of great excitement.

My friend John Ayling and me had cycled from Dover and were some 70 miles away from home camped in a field next door to a farm house. The couple living there were kind enough to provide us with hot water and milk to make some tea. The farmer was intently listening to the wireless, listening to the commentators as they waited for further results to come through. An unexpected lead started to build up for the Labour Party. It was obvious that the men coming home from the war had decided to put their trust in Mr Attlee and his Labour Party. There was a great breakthrough in Dover when the first Labour candidate for Dover was elected as Member of Parliament. He was a Mr Thomas and remained in office for the next 4 years.

The Labour Party were virtually thrust into power with a huge majority and the public expected them to provide a land fit for heroes. Billy Newman, a founder member of the Dover Labour Party in the 1920s and for many years chairman of the Dover District Labour Party, and secretary of the powerful Tilmanstone Miners Union, had worked hard for this day.

For him it was a time of jubilation. The members of the Labour Party had held firm to their beliefs. They had remained loyal to their cause and now victory had been their reward. The mines were taken into public ownership. The railways and steelworks were nationalised. The power-house of the country became accountable to the government. Under the energetic and imaginative direction of Nye Bevan, the National Health Service was established which has lasted over 60 years and more, to this present day.

Chapter 53

The Gravesend Bye Election And Corruption.

The Labour government had its disappointments as well as its great successes. It possessed a very strong leadership composed of powerful and imaginative personalities. It included members of wide practical experience and strong intellect, but like most large scale organisations, it had its problems.

Hugh Dalton was the most prominent personality to hit the headlines when, as Chancellor, he leaked information to the press relating to the forthcoming budget. His was a purely personal and political misjudgement. For this he immediately resigned his post as Chancellor of the Exchequer. However, he still played a prominent role in the inner circles of government and in the upper echelons of the Labour Party.

Two further cases were more serious since they concerned matters of personal integrity. A junior minister, Mr Belcher failed to register a gift he had received in his position as Minister and as a result was asked to give up his ministerial post.

Mr Garry Allingham, an ex-journalist, was Member of Parliament for Gravesend, in Kent. Sometime after he had been elected it was reported that he had absconded with the party funds and had gone abroad. A parliamentary vacancy occurred and a bye-election was declared.

The story of this misdemeanour filled the press headlines with talk of corruption within the Labour Party. It was incumbent on the Labour Party to provide a candidate at the forthcoming bye-election of pristine character. The candidate selected was Sir Richard Ackland, a respected politician and a minister of the church.

A date for the election was set and the campaign on both sides started with vigour and determination. A great deal was made by association with Garry Allingham and his activities. He was portrayed as a corrupt kind of person that made up the Labour Party. Emotions ran high, but on the ground

Labour supporters appeared apathetic. Labour canvassers who knocked on doors were finding very little interest or support for the Party. It appeared that the Conservative message of Labour corruption and incompetence was getting home.

The Labour Party Central Office became worried and looked for ways that might in some way engender an interest amongst the voters. A message came through to Billy Newman in Dover seeking his advice and help. It was agreed that he, with his own team of miners, help with a week's canvass in Gravesend and that Billy would chair the 'eve of poll' meeting at the Market Hall. Each day that week Billy organised a bus load of Tilmanstone miners to travel to Gravesend to canvass known Labour areas and visit the pubs to try and whip up a little enthusiasm among the voters.

On the eve of poll I drove up with my father to Gravesend. It was evening and it was dark. We parked the car and I was told to go straight to the Market Hall and father would meet me there after the close of the meeting. When I asked where he was going he said to the pubs to collect the men before they drink too much!

When I arrived at the Hall, a large market hall, it was already three-quarters full, mostly with people standing. There were already some hundreds of people there. It appeared that the canvassers had done their bit, that their magic had worked. Besides the galaxy of talent amongst the speakers on the platform, it had been made known that the Miners Male Voice Choir would be there in full voice. The Hall rapidly filled and it appeared that this vast crowd numbered some 500 or more people. It was the biggest I had seen at a public meeting. There was a great deal of chattering. The noise of voices filled that great hall, when suddenly a light flashed on the stage and a voice boomed out,

"Friends! Comrades! Pray Silence! ---- The Miners are coming!"

and with that the voices of the Miners Choir burst forth singing that great Welsh hymn, the Cwm-Rhondda! One by one, in single file, the Miners Choir moved forward from the rear of the hall. Slowly the vast crowd moved to make way for these men as they moved majestically through the darkened hall toward the stage. Each man was guided by the torch like lamp affixed to his miner's helmet and the crowd closed ranks behind them with a growing sound of applause that quickly filled the hall.

The spotlight was on the Chairman as the members of the choir lined the stage. It was a magnificent display of showmanship which aroused the crowd to an excited demonstration of appreciation from all corners of the hall.

The Chairman, a man of small stocky build, somehow in that dazzling light conveyed an imposing manner. He took off his workingman's cap, screwed it up in his hand and waited a second, then with that most powerful voice, his words rang out across the hall.

"Ladies and Gentlemen, Friends! Comrades! This is a Great Day! This is Your Day!

"You! by Your Action, will make known, the kind of government you want!

"You will make known the kind of country in which you wish to live!

"Many of you, men and women have been fighting for the very survival of this country. Sadly many of your friends will never return. They are among those thousands who have fallen on the battlefields of Europe.

"The vote in the General Election told us clearly the kind of society they wished for! This is what they fought for! A land of fairness! A rich country in talent and spirit, where there is plenty for all!

"Ladies and Gentlemen! Comrades, do not betray their trust! Keep faith with them! Do what is right!

"Comrades! Here on the stage are miners from Tilmanstone in Kent who, during the day work hard producing coal, coal for the power stations, coal for industry and coal to heat our homes.

"These men are like you.

"They are no different except that for most of the light of the day, they are in the dark, working by artificial light. They are down below, a thousand feet below ground, working in tunnels, hot, sweaty, and often waist deep in water.

"They are no different from many of you. They are blacksmiths, carpenters, electricians, winders, machine operators.

"They rely on each other for their safety, so we work together. We keep faith with each other.

"Comrades all!

"Let each one of us in this Hall tonight pledge to do what is right! Let us keep faith with our fellow citizens!"

"Potatoes? Potatoes!"

"Did someone shout out potato rationing? Yes! We have potato rationing!

"Would you sooner see some go hungry, while you feast with your friends at the table?

"Maybe you would, but I know I wouldn't, and I know most of you people here tonight would not like to be associated with that gentleman. Where there are shortages let us share fairly what we have!

"Ladies and Gentlemen,

"Comrades, enjoy the evening, with the Choir singing those wonderful words of Blake's 'Jerusalem!'

The Chairman introduced a galaxy of talent including some prominent Cabinet Ministers to speak on behalf of the candidate, Sir Richard Ackland. The evening ended with the choir and audience raising the roof with a rousing rendition of "Land of Hope and Glory".

The Chairman bade everybody goodnight and wished all a safe journey home.

The next day Sir Richard Ackland was proclaimed the victor. The Labour Party had retained the seat. The people were well pleased. Billy Newman received a number of phone calls offering congratulations and expressing appreciation at the fine performance of the choir.

Some days later we had a pleasant surprise when father received a letter from Downing Street. It was eagerly opened and there was a hand written letter from Clement Attlee, the Prime Minister and leader of the Labour Party, thanking Billy Newman for his great contribution that had helped to make the by-election at Gravesend such a success.

Chapter 54

Kingsway Hall. World Government.

Time progressed, and in 1949 I was a student in my first year, attending the London School of Economics, just off Kingsway.

One afternoon I crossed over the road to Kingsway Hall to look at the notices in the window. One Notice took my particular interest. It was a notice advertising a meeting pertaining to the notion of "World Government". Since I was reading the Social Sciences and Politics under among others the famed Professor Harold Laski, this subject appeared most relevant to my studies. As I looked down the notice I read the names of some famous people including Sir William Beveridge, the Rev Donald Soper, Claude Bourdet "a former member of the French Resistance in Paris" and now Editor of the left wing newspaper Combat.

The star of the show was the American wartime bomber pilot Garry Davis, who had been so greatly influenced by all he saw and all that he had done during the war, that he gave up his passport, renounced his American citizenship and declared himself a citizen of the world. He applied to the United Nations whilst in Paris for "World Citizenship". The United Nations representatives replied that it could not give it to him, since they were not a world government, and had no powers to grant such a request. The French government, out of respect for his integrity and his immense popularity in France, allowed him to remain in Paris without papers.

I decided I would go to this meeting. The title and the list of speakers provided an attraction not to be missed. It was a fine evening and crowds of people were beginning to fill the hall. I found a seat near the back and waited for the speakers to find their way to the platform.

I had no foreknowledge what to expect. To my great surprise, almost consternation, the man sitting there, on the platform in the spotlight, was none other than Billy Newman, my father!

He then stood and introduced himself as one humble citizen, a working coalminer from a pit in Kent, but with him during the course of the evening they would be introduced to a galaxy of personalities from all walks of life. "This evening you will be privileged to be entertained by the Tilmanstone Male Voice Choir, the Miners Choir from Kent. So ladies and gentlemen let the evening begin with that great Welsh Hymn, the Cym-Rhondda!"

The meeting ended with a rousing rendition by the Choir with the singing of Jerusalem as the miners walked off stage to loud applause. The meeting had been a great success.

Sometime later a conference and fete took place at Chelmsford. I was too busy with my studies at LSE, attending lectures and seminars and was unable to be at the Conference, but I still have the programme dated June 24th-25th 1949.

The Conference took place over a full week. People such as Lord Boyd Orr, Lord Beveridge, and Albert Einstein, etc acted as sponsors for this People's World Convention. This campaign was linked with campaigns in France, Denmark and Belgium.

To quote Lord Beveridge,

"World government will not be easy to establish. But not one of you can have the security of a peaceful life without it... I hope that everyone who reads this will decide to study and support as I do, the practical plan of the Crusade for World Government."

During a foreign affairs debate, in the House of Commons, as early as November 1945, Ernest Bevin, Foreign Secretary is quoted as saying,

"We need a new study for the purpose of creating a World Assembly elected directly by the people of the world. I am willing to sit with anybody of any party, of any nation, to try to devise a franchise or constitution for a World Assembly. Once we have got to that stage I believe we shall have taken a great progressive step."

Among people listed as speakers at the various meetings during the week were Lord Boyd Orr, DSO, LlD, FRS, one time Director of the Food and Agricultural Organisation of the United Nations, Claude Bourdet who fought with the French Resistance, was arrested by the Gestapo and sent to Oranienburg concentration camp and later to Buchenwald. He later served as Director-General of the French broadcasting service. In 1947, he took over the editorship of the newspaper Combat.

Further speakers listed included Alderman William Newman JP, Secretary of the Tilmanstone Branch Kent Mine Workers' Association, 1918-1946 and President of the Kent Mine Workers' Association 1921-1933. He was elected as a County Councillor in 1938 and in 1946 became a County Alderman. He was appointed a magistrate in 1930. All this time, he earned his living underground, as a working miner, digging out coal.

Another notable member taking part was Dr Cyril Joad, an indefatigable worker for progressive causes, who was Head of the Department of Philosophy and Psychology at Birkbeck College, London University. He became well known as a resident member of the BBC Brain's Trust. The Tilmanstone (Kent) Colliery Male Voice Choir was listed as leading the community singing entitled Music from the Mines at the Corn Exchange. There were a great deal of other activities listed on the programme.

SOME OF THE PEOPLE
WHO WILL SPEAK

LORD BOYD ORR, D.S.O., LL.D., F.R.S., who from his early days has been a research worker, was M.P. for Scottish Universities in 1945-46, and Chancellor of Glasgow University in 1946. He is a member of the Colonial Advisory Council of Agriculture and Animal Health, and of the Advisory Committee of Nutrition, Ministry of Health. He recently retired from the Directorship of the Food and Agriculture Organisation of the United Nations, and was elected President of the World Movement for World Federal Government at Luxembourg this year. He is president, among other organisations, of the National Peace Council and of the International Friendship League, and a member of the National Executive Council of the Crusade for World Government.

The Imam (Arabic for priest) of Woking— DR. S. MUHAMMED ABDULLAH, Ph.D., the leading Moslem in this country and editor of the *Islamic Review*.

MRS. JAI KISHORI HANDOO, is a leading Indian social worker, at present in this country.

CLAUDE BOURDET, engineer and journalist spoke English before he spoke French. He was educated in France and Switzerland and then took up a Government post as a specialist in scientific management. During the war he served as an artillery officer until he was demobilized in 1940, when he joined the " Combat " resistance group. He was arrested by the Gestapo in 1944 and sent to Oranienburg concentration camp and later to Buchenwald. On his return to France in 1945 he was elected Vice-President of the Provisional Consultative Assembly, and later became director-general of the French broadcasting service. In January, 1947, he took over the editorship of the newspaper *Combat* which he had run when it was an " underground " newspaper.

ALDERMAN WILLIAM NEWMAN, J.P., has been a miner all his working life. He entered the pits as a boy of 13 in Yorkshire and went to Kent in 1917. He began work at the Tilmanstone Colliery in August of that year and became Secretary of the Tilmanstone branch Kent Mine Workers' Association in 1918 a post he held until 1946. He was President of his union from 1921 to 1933. In May 1918, Mr. Newman was elected a Kent County Councillor and in November 1946, Alderman. He was appointed J.P. in 1930.

DR. CYRIL JOAD, born in London in 1891, educated at Blundell's and Oxford, has for long been one of the foremost advocates of a Federal World Government and an indefatigable worker for progressive causes. He was once a civil servant, but retired in 1930 to head the department of Philosophy and Psychology at Birkbeck College, London University. He first broadcast in 1937 and was a resident member of the B.B.C. Brains Trust. He has been Chairman of the National Peace Council and has written numerous books and pamphlets.

RICHARD WRIGHT, famous negro author of the American classic " Black Boy," a story about racial prejudice, and one of America's leading advocates of equality for coloured peoples.

HENRY C. USBORNE, Member of Parliament for Acocks Green, Birmingham, since 1945, is a Managing Director of Nu-way Heating Plants Ltd., Birmingham. He is also a Vice-President of Federal Union and of the National Peace Council, and the Hon. General Secretary and member of the National Council of the Crusade for World Government.

13

Though the Conference was looked upon as a success, in that it brought to public attention the importance of working together for World peace, the idea of making a reality of World government was as far away as ever. Those years were dominated by the formation of the United Nations, the Bretton-Woods discussions on world finance, and the ideological conflict between the Soviet Union and the West resulting as a consequence in the establishment of the Atlantic Pact, the North Atlantic Treaty Organisation. Despite the valiant efforts of the dedicated few, who never wavered in their beliefs, for the general public the thought of world government receded into the shadows.

Chapter 55

The Korean War and Vietnam.
The Spread of Communism in the East.

It appeared as though clouds of darkness were once more enveloping the world. There was the Korean War, in which the Chinese supported the Communists in the north while the Americans and British supported the south in what proved to be a bloody, ideological contest, with threats of it spreading into a nuclear conflict.

Then followed the uprising in Vietnam, led by Fu-Chi-Ming who succeeded, after much fierce fighting, in driving out the French from their last colonial fortress in Dien Bien Phu and prepared for an advance southward to take over the rest of the country. The Americans fearing the spread of Communisn across the whole of South-East Asia sent some 200 thousand troops to prevent any further incursions in this area. They found, however, that these revolutionary forces were far more effective than they anticipated. The Americans used what can only be described as terror tactics by using napalm bombs which set people alight and chemical agents dropped on mass bombing raids over the forests with the intention of destroying all life, including the trees, and leaving the country a waste land.

In spite of overwhelming military might of the United States the rebels proved determined and tactically superior, the Americans suffering defeat after defeat until they were forced to leave the country.

In Europe the generous help provided by America, at the instigation of that wise American Statesman, General Marshal, enabled the rebuilding of Germany, which had suffered so much destruction as a result of the tactics of Bomber Harris, known as "carpet bombing". However Marshal's most wonderful accomplishment was increasingly overshadowed by the powerful and dangerous threat inherent in the Cold War. America and Russia were building ever more powerful military machines.

The development of long range rockets fixed with nuclear warheads were seen as a danger to the survival of the world. Large groups of people in all countries formed pressure groups, joined in mass demonstrations protesting at the use of nuclear arms. Their cry was for unilateral nuclear disarmament and was lead in this country by the likes of Michael Foot, philosopher Bertrand Russell, the Reverend Bruce Kent and many other leaders of the church.

There were well organised demonstrations. In London there were marches supported by thousands ending in mass gatherings in Hyde Park. A sit down demonstration filled Trafalgar Square and among those were people including Bertrand Russell an international figure and local people, well respected figures from Dover. The thousands of people, represented a real cross-section of the population. These demonstrations were of great significance, in that they brought to public attention the great danger of nuclear war.

It was through these tumultuous times that my father lived. First the Boer War, then the Great War of 1914-1918, and latterly the World War 1939-1945. It was from the times of the horse drawn carriages, the coming of the motorcar, and now the aeroplane. His mind was indelibly affected by these experiences, yet he still believed that people working together with these great scientific and technological achievements could achieve something better, a better world.

Chapter 56

David Ennals and Dick Knowles.

My Father was still very active and played a great part in the election of the second Labour Party representative for Dover, to the House of Commons, a Mr David Ennals. I have a photo of my father with David Ennals, in conversation with Frank Cousins, leader of the Transport and General Workers Union at a meeting in Dover. The labour party agent at the time was a person called Dick Knowles whom I used to drive around, taking him to Labour Party meetings on wet and windy nights, to the out-lying villages in the Dover area. Sometimes the village halls were almost empty with just a half dozen supporters. However whatever the number, however small the attendance, we felt it worthwhile. Each person to us, was of equal importance.

Billy talking to Transport and General Workers leader Frank Cousins (right) talking to David Ennals (centre).

It was on a visit to Birmingham many years later when I was Chairman of Finance on Dover District Council that I once again met Dick Knowles. The Finance Officer of Dover District Council and myself were attending a Conference organised by "Investment and Financial Advisors", for the purpose of obtaining the latest information relating to financial dealings with Local Authorities. Our advisors included U.B.S. Phillips and Drew.

The Lord Mayor of Birmingham was acting as host to those attending the Conference. He was none other than Dick Knowles, one time Labour Party Agent in Dover. I could hardly believe it.

I went round to the Offices of the City Council and asked the receptionist if it would be possible to see Sir Richard. She replied that it was impossible as he had a full time table that day. I tried again at lunch time. This time I asked the receptionist if she would give him my card, on which I wrote Billy Newman from Dover, son of Billy Newman, Tilmanstone Colliery. A message came back, "see you at 5 O'clock for quarter of an hour."

I returned to the Conference Hall and met my friend, the finance officer, Richard Bowditch and invited him to accompany me to meet the Lord Mayor of Birmingham. We arrived precisely on time and were taken up to the Mayor's Chamber.

The door opened and Sir Richard jumped out of his chair, greeting us with outstretched hands and the words, "A vision from the past. You haven't changed a bit! I would have recognised you anywhere. They were great times!" And turning to address my friend, he said, "But you should have seen his father, now there was a man, an exceptional man. On a Friday he would sit at his table on the pit top collecting Union Dues. We were both wanting to recruit more members to the Labour Party, so he invited me as Agent to get a table with labour party leaflets and membership cards and he would encourage any of his Union Members to see me."

The sun was shining, and we were having a good day. When over the crest of the pit top approached six men, in their city suits, on their way to the Manager's office. The pits had been nationalised and the pits were looked upon as government property. Some MPs felt they had a particular relationship as between the pits and the government. One such person was the then right wing Tony Benn! He broke away from the rest of the group and approached the Labour Party Agent Dick Knowles and after greeting him said, "Do you know that you are not allowed to do this on government property and that you might be prosecuted? I think it might be wise for you to move from coal-board property!"

Dick Knowles replied, "Sir, the decision to be here is not mine. I'm just carrying out instructions. You would be advised to speak to the man at the other table, but I'd be careful how you approach the subject. He's Billy Newman the Union Leader and if you don't want the wheels of this pit to stop turning, tread a little carefully. Pleased to meet you Mr Benn." Mr Benn thanked him and went and had a word with Billy Newman enquiring about the morale of the men and their relationship with the management. And so the day ended, very much as it had begun. They were memorable times. They were great days.

It was thus that we said good-bye to Sir Richard, now a Knight of the Realm, completely dressed for the part. He was now rather portly and wore a decorative waistcoat, black tie and tails, of Pickwickian demeanour.

When we were outside, Richard Bowditch the Director of Finance of Dover District Council turned to me and said, "You know Councillor Newman, that's been a most interesting conversation. It's not often you hear such stories at first hand. You ought to copy it down, write about it for the record. You know you're not getting any younger!"

I thought to myself, you're being very supportive! I could see he was exuding that spirit of optimism and I thought that there's time yet! And so we returned to our hotel, the end of a perfect day.

During this period of his later years, from the late 1940s to the 1960s, Billy Newman was as active as ever he had been. His main activities centred round the changing nature of the aims and objectives of the Union. Safety, health, welfare and the furthering of leisure activities were assuming a greater importance as policy objectives. With the tragic loss of Tilden Smith and the establishment of a bureaucratic organisation of nationalisation the relations between management and union had to be forged all over again. Nationalisation brought with it difficulties and disappointments as well as advantages. At Tilmanstone, an Admiral was put in charge of the Regional Coal Board at Dover. He was responsible for general management at Tilmanstone. Not used to the rough and tumble of Union politics he did not welcome the advice of Union Officials. He was an administrator carrying out government policy and he was in charge.

I well remember father on the telephone requesting a meeting to discuss certain matters of policy. Father held out the receiver from his ear and I could hear the voice at the other end shouting down the phone, "I am in charge! I've told you once Newman this is none of your business and if you keep this up, I'll break you if it's the last thing I do." Sometime later Billy got his meeting!

Chapter 57

Meeting with Doctors.

Billy kept up his work with the local doctors, Dr Bellamy at Eythorne, and Dr Fraser at Eastry, but more than this he kept up his good personal relations with a number of the leading medical professionals in London. Twice I had personal experience of his associations with such people.

The first time was when I was returning to Ebbw Vale during the war. I would be about 14 years of age. Father accompanied me to London where he said he had some business. He had always had a deep interest in the nature of skin diseases which were associated with working down the pit. Billy had made friends with a French specialist in matters relating to the skin. He was Dr Assen who had a practice in Harley Street, London. As far as my father was concerned he always gave advice to him free, no charge, in fact he was always pleased to see him.

We arrived in London with some time to spare before my train would depart from Paddington so father decided to take me with him to Harley Street. We were met by the Receptionist who took us to the waiting room and soon Dr Assen came in, and with a warm welcoming smile, greeted us both. I was introduced and made to feel very much at ease. Father explained that I was off back to school in South Wales. Dr Assen asked what I intended to do when I left school and if I wished to take up medicine as a career he would be pleased to take me on as a trainee prior to attending Medical School. I thanked him very much, but needless to say I never took up the offer. I then left father to his business and walked down to Paddington Station to catch the train for Wales.

My second experience was, some years later, when I was working in London. Father was coming up that Saturday morning to visit Sir Ambrose Woodhall, the Doctor in charge of Manor House Hospital. I took this opportunity to meet my father for a cup of tea and a chat. He suggested I meet him outside the hospital and we would arrange our day.

Father said he had a timed appointment with Sir Ambrose which shouldn't last more than half an hour so it would be best if I would come in and wait inside. This I did and was ushered to a seat outside the Office where they were meeting. I sat and read the newspaper, and at the said time father emerged with Sir Ambrose who introduced himself by telling me what a pleasure it was to meet a son of Billy Newman. As it happened I had a slight growth on my throat and my father said to Sir Ambrose, "Do you think anything might be done about this? The local Doctor doesn't seem to think so!"

Sir Ambrose had a brief look and said, "It doesn't look very pretty! Yes, I think we could do something. Come across to this Office at 11 o'clock on Wednesday morning and we will see what we can do."

This I did and met his Secretary, who invited me to sit down and said that Sir Ambrose would not be long. I waited for some time, when the Secretary returned and said she was very sorry but Sir Ambrose was assisting at an operation and would be sometime yet, but he would be grateful if I could wait and see him in some 30 minutes.

I thought he just wanted to have a chat!

It was near dinner time and I had gone without breakfast so I went across to the canteen and bought a sandwich. I was a little hungry! I returned to the Secretary's office and sat and waited.

The young lady came out occasionally and apologised for the fact that I had to wait all this time, but she emphasised that Sir Ambrose would like to see me if it was convenient. It was now past dinner time and I assumed that all he wanted to do was to talk and nothing more.

It was about 1 o'clock when the Secretary excitedly spoke to me saying that Sir Ambrose could see me now. I followed her along the corridor where two doors swung open, and much to my amazement a trolley was wheeled out with a body resting on it. A few seconds later two men came out dressed in all their surgical regalia, in the act of taking off their face masks. The shorter of the two, Sir Ambrose, approached me and said how sorry he was that it had been necessary for me to wait so long but he would see what could be done.

He turned to his companion, a surgeon, Mr Nicholson, and said could he spare ten minutes and do him a favour. They took me into a spare room full of medical equipment where, after some quiet conversation and feeling round my throat, Dr Nicholson acceded to Sir Ambrose request.

The lady anaesthetist said she was willing to help, where upon she asked me if I had had anything to eat. When I said yes, but just a sandwich, she was adamant and refused the request to give me an anaesthetic. Sir Ambrose turned to Dr Nicholson and after some muttering and probing my neck, nodded to one another, and said "a local!"

"Yes, a local!"

A nurse came and ushered me into the theatre and politely asked me to take off my shoes and with a smile said that it was just a precaution in case I started kicking! And then to really put me at my ease she requested that I take my shirt off with the words,

"Well we wouldn't want you to have blood all over your nice clean shirt, would we? Now climb on the operating table and lie down!"

A few minutes later Dr Nicholson, in all his medical costume, leaned over me, felt round the lump in my neck when the nurse handed him a syringe. He said, "Now you will feel a slight prick, but nothing more," and he proceeded to insert the needle into my throat. "Now that didn't hurt, just once more," and he proceeded to insert the needle several times.

After a few moments he continued by telling me that he would proceed with the main task of removing the cyst. He had to take care because he did not want to damage any of the muscles in my throat. He said, "I am about to make an incision into your throat. There will be a little blood but there's no need to be alarmed." I lay there with my mouth firmly closed ensuring that I would not make any movement that might upset the actions of the surgeon. A voice from above said, "How's your Father?"

I thought he can't be talking to me, when the voice repeated, "How's your father?"

I tried without moving my mouth to say, "Are you talking to me?" The voice replied with a slight touch of humour, "Who do you think I'm talking to? Now how's your father?"

"You can open your mouth you know, it won't affect anything I am doing!" And so we continued the conversation.

When he had finished, Dr Nicholson and the Sister tried to persuade me to go to bed and have a few days rest at the hospital but, being perhaps a little too stubborn for my own good, I insisted on leaving and returned to my lodgings in Tottenham. I was told to return in three days' time to have my neck checked over. The whole proceedings proved successful and I thanked Dr Nicholson for the consideration and kindness he had displayed toward me. I asked him to convey my best wishes and thanks to all those staff who had given their spare time to help in the operation.

A few days later I returned home to Eythorne and told my mother all that had happened. She replied," They'd do anything for your Dad!" And so it was that father had built up such a close relationship with these people, who provided so much help in dealing with the medical problems encountered by the workmen at the pit. The friendships made went far beyond the call of duty or what was laid down in a contract.

The many friendships Billy Newman had made remained strong throughout his lifetime. Regular visitors included Syd Dye who, in 1945 became a Member of Parliament and was a close friend of Hugh Gaitskell, Dr Mabel Tylecote who had served as Lord Mayor of Manchester, Miss Leak who founded a school in South Africa and was helped financially by Lady Nancy Astor, Miss Jan Macdonald, and Dr George Bell, Bishop of Chichester, among many others.

It was after one of Miss Leaks visits that I remember we received a card from Lady Astor inviting us to tea at her home in Sandwich Bay. That was in 1950.

Billy Newman continued to work actively for the Labour Party, and gave support to various prospective candidates, including Bill Owen, and Jack Lee. It was some years later that David Ennals became the Parliamentary candidate and Member of Parliament for Dover. Visitors to the constituency supporting the Labour candidate and addressing public meetings, included a more accomplished Tony Benn, Dennis Healey, Frank Cousins and the leader of the Labour Party, Harold Wilson.

David Ennals, the Labour candidate held the seat for 6 years until 1970 when the Conservatives, with Peter Rees as their candidate, regained the seat. The Conservatives maintained their supremacy for some 27 years, Peter Rees for 17 years, followed by David Shaw for 10 years. It was at this time that a friend of mine, Mr Gwyn Prosser, was elected as Member of Parliament for Dover. Serving for some 13 years, he became the longest serving Labour MP for Dover.

Chapter 58

Billy Retires as Secretary of Union.
Offers from Management.

Billy Newman was giving a great deal of his time to his public works as a Magistrate and serving on several Committees of the County Council during the war years. In 1945 with the advent of the Labour government under Prime Minister, Major Clement Attlee, the coal mines were taken out of private hands and placed into public ownership. This had been a prime objective of the Labour Party ever since the setting up of the Sankey Commission in 1919.

Now at the age of 61, Billy felt it time to resign as Secretary of Tilmanstone Union. So after some 26 years as an activist at the centre of the rough and tumble of Union affairs, Billy retired.

Some days later, after he had made his intentions known, Billy received a letter from Mr G. Hannaford, a Director of Tilmanstone (Kent) Collieries Limited, offering him the position of Rehabilitation Officer for a period of five years at a salary of £6 per week. Billy thanked him for the kind offer, but said he would continue to work on the surface for the next few years in order to qualify for the pension which working miners were to receive after nationalisation. This he had to do in order to receive a pension, for the scheme was based on the contributory principle.

A number of years later when we were travelling back from Maidstone my father asked me if I would mind us stopping off at Canterbury Hospital. He had heard that Mr Hare, the Area Colliery Manager, was not too well and felt he ought to pay him a visit. I was somewhat surprised, since though he was unwell, he had for many years represented the management at Tilmanstone Colliery and had strongly opposed much of what my father, as Union representative, demanded and indeed fought for. I thought he was the last person he would visit.

When I expressed my thoughts father said to me with a certain amount of severity, "Look young man, just because someone disagrees with you, and may even oppose everything you stand for, it doesn't make them any less a human being!" and so we made our way to Canterbury Hospital.

I had a coffee and duly waited in the reception area for my father. We later proceeded to the car and went on our way home. When safely out on the main road I asked father how the visit went. He told me that Mr Hare was both surprised and pleased to see him. There was no doubt he was seriously ill, though he was quite cheerful.

They had an interesting chat about the old days and when my father commented on the success he had achieved for the men as Union representative, of which he was justly proud, he wondered sometimes whether he had sacrificed too much personally. He could have made a great deal of money working for the management! He had received several offers from both management and the insurance company.

Mr Hare replied, "Don't ever change Billy! The one thing I most greatly respected you for was the fact that however hard we fought each other, you always played it with a straight bat. Don't ever change." A tribute indeed. Billy now devoted most of his time to his work as a County Councillor representing Eastry South.

Chapter 59

Social Class. The Appointment of Magistrates.

1945 was indeed a turning point. It was marked by the end of the war in Europe and the General Election in which Mr Clement Attlee and the Labour Party were swept to power. His government included a determined group, men of vision, but they were beginning to show fatigue, having served in government throughout the War.

The men coming home, having seen and endured so much suffering, were determined to seek a change. Men and Officers, regardless of rank joined together in the movements pressing for a better life, and a better world. They joined in active politics. They made their views known. Some joined the Communist Party, but larger numbers supported Attlee's Labour Party. New Parties were formed, including the Commonwealth Party under the leadership of Sir Richard Ackland.

The Liberals pre-1914 and the Conservatives since 1920 had been the major political parties assured of majorities, providing them with sufficient power to govern the country. During that time society was imbued with traditional conservative values particularly relating to status and class.

Total war, with its closeness of relationships, men dependent for their very survival on one another, had softened the edges of class division. Questions which came to mind, were not, "Who are you? Where do you come from?" They were rather, "Can I rely on him to watch my back! Is he reliable?"

However, even to this day, class division still exists, particularly in the more important and influential spheres of life, "The exercise of power." The form may have changed, but these groups of people still exist, surrounded by barriers as strong as ever. Membership is not necessarily formal, but one of acceptance and recognition. "You are one of us! You are now one of the Establishment!"

In 1945, with a Labour government in power, the modest changes in attitudes of people to one another regardless of class may have appeared an epic break with the past, and so it was in many ways.

In 1945 and 1950 the mines were brought into public ownership. They were nationalised. The recommendations of the Beveridge Report creating the basis of the welfare state were implemented. The education system was restructured to form, it was hoped, a fairer system of opportunity for the youth of this country. The National Health Service was established, owing much to the fiery energy and determination of Aneurin Bevan. To quote Beveridge, "this was a time for triumph and rejoicing."

Up till this time, the Union and the local mining community had been Billy Newman's life. The house had been a meeting place of friends. The door was always open with a welcoming smile and a warm cup of tea. It formed the centre for a close circle of friends sharing ideas and information. Now with the greater part of his time taken up with County Council activities and public service work Billy was out much of the time. He travelled about a good deal more, spending much of his time in Maidstone, at the County Council Offices, some 40 miles away. The relationship with those people he met in the course of this work was less tight. Though the members and officers were friendly there was not that close bond that existed in the mining community. Problems appeared to be more general, less immediate. In spite of all the differences between them, Billy appeared to have been accepted by this solid phalanx of Conservative Councillors from the wealthier sections of the county.

Billy's beliefs remained the same. He remained an ardent Socialist. He believed that with drive and determination he could rise to any occasion. He was fearless and could be truly challenging whatever the status of those he confronted. This is well illustrated in the altercation he had concerning the appointment of magistrates with the Lord Lieutenant of Kent, Lord Cornwallis.

Meetings were held every so often to appoint Magistrates. Father was a member of the Kent County Appointments Committee which was chaired by Lord Cornwallis. There was one vacancy to be filled in the rural area including the villages of Elvington and Eythorne. From a number of competing recommendations the Committee, with the support of the Lord Lieutenant, agreed with Mr Newman's recommendation that Mr David Jenkins of Elvington be appointed. The decision was unanimous. All that remained was for Mr Jenkins to be appointed as a Magistrate of the Wingham Bench.

Mr Jenkins was a member of the Management at Tilmanstone Colliery and in no way could he be considered a miner. He was the Finance Officer for the Management and had held that position for many years. He and my father represented opposing interests and had experienced many violent clashes relating to the miners' interests, but this did not blind my father to the fact that Mr Jenkins did much social work in the mining village of Elvington where Mr Jenkins lived. He worked with the wardens of the Settlement and one of the ventures he is remembered for was the organisation of Saturday morning film shows for children which were held in the Village Hall.

A few days after the meeting of the Appointments Committee father received a letter from the Lord Lieutenant's Office stating that there was to be a change of the appointment to the Wingham Bench and that a decision had been made by the members of the committee and supported by Lord Cornwallis, the Lord Lieutenant, and all that remained was for Mr Newman to agree. The proposition was that instead of Mr Jenkins being appointed Mr Harman-Hunt, Manager of Guildford Estate, would henceforth fill the vacancy representing Elvington and Eythorne. They would welcome his reply at the earliest opportunity in order to confirm this decision.

Mr Newman replied with the brief statement that he stuck by the original decision of the Committee, to which all had agreed, that Mr Jenkins be appointed.

A second letter was received, more friendly in its tone but emphasising that all members of the committee had agreed to the change and it just remained for Mr Newman to give his assent and the matter would be closed.

The reply from Billy Newman was that he still held to the former decision that Mr Jenkins be appointed.

A few days later I drove father to Maidstone to attend one of his Council meetings. He was met on the steps of County Hall by the Clerk to the Magistrates. The Clerk in those days had much the same powers as the Chief Executive today. He greeted my father and they went into a private room and had a discussion.

After the Council meeting ended I met my father and drove him home, some 40 miles to Eythorne. On the way we talked about things in general but I could not resist asking him what the meeting with the Clerk to the Council was all about. It must have been something important. Were they proposing that he take up a more important post on the Council? The answer was no. The meeting which was in private and off the record.

"Did I have anything against Mr Harman-Hunt?" to which he had replied, "No." The Clerk pursued the matter by asking if there were a vacancy and he was appointed would he make a good magistrate. My father's reply was an unequivocal yes. The Clerk then said that of course this was off the record and all supposition, but if there were two vacancies on the Wingham Bench and one of the recommendations was Mr Harman-Hunt would my father oppose it. My father's reply was that he would not oppose such a proposition providing Mr Jenkins was the first appointment. Some days later the appointments were announced.

Some weeks later Billy Newman saw a letter from the Chairman of the Wingham Bench sent to the Lord Lieutenant which caused all the trouble. It stated that he, the Chairman of Wingham Bench, already had one miner on his Bench and he was determined that there should not be another, referring to Mr Jenkins. He stated in unequivocal terms that Mr

Harman-Hunt should be appointed. He did a lot of good work for Lady Guildford as Manager of her Estate, and besides they went hunting together and he was a very good companion.

It so happened that Mr Jenkins lived in the village and was thus most easily accessible to those who might require his services, whereas Mr Harman Hunt lived some distance 3 to 5 miles away across the parkland.

My father was the miner to whom the Chairman of the Bench was alluding. Little did he know that this miner sat on the Appointments Committee. To father this was little more than class prejudice and demonstrated its influence in high places. It is clearly evident if one looks up the names of those who have served as Chairmen of the Bench that it exists right up to the present day.

The fact that the Lord Lieutenant is the Chairman of the Appointments Committee tells its own story. To this day, how many people know of such positions of authority as the Lieutenancy that are organised throughout the Country, represented with their entourage of Deputy Lieutenants.

Chapter 60

The Challenges faced after 1945.

The post-war period from 1945 was a very different place from that which preceded the war. Both the industrial and political landscapes had radically altered, bringing forth new challenges. The enduring beliefs associated with the respect for persons embodied in those words "Liberty, Equality and Fraternity" were still there. The vision which had been held for so long and sharpened by the experience of the war remained, but for many people these ideals receded into the background as their lives were affected by social and economic change. They were superseded by the more immediate demands made possible by developments in technology, of consumption and the media. Advertising has become a fact of life. It reaches out and affects all we do. How much can I buy? How much profit can I make? Equality is forgotten, fraternity weakened and liberty is held to justify the changed values. The new slogan is "Choice! Freedom of Choice!" And the nature of that choice is provided by the advertising companies and political commentators.

The Unions
Trades Unions were to some extent a victim of their own success. A great deal of what they had stood for appears to have been achieved. This combined with the fact that many disputes became depicted as an attack on the government rather than a claim against an employer. This made large sections of the public think that the Unions had become too powerful, a danger to the state. There was a growing feeling that laws should be introduced to limit their powers. Not only was business enthusiastic about such ideas, but they were supported by Members of Parliament, government Ministers and they were being given voice too, by large numbers of the general public. It was a strong force, and this, with the advent of television when news and comment were soon to be projected into every home and repeated daily, it was difficult if not impossible to resist.

Chapter 61

Billy's latter days in the Pit. County Council Activities.

Election as an Alderman of K.C.C.
Billy resigned as Union Secretary in 1946, having served some 28 years in that position, since he was first elected in 1918. He remained working at the pit for some years later in order to qualify for a pit pension. You may have worked underground, hewing coal in most difficult conditions, year after year, but unless you still worked after the mines were actually

nationalised and paid a contribution, you received no pension. The amount of pension you received was based on the number of contributions you had made.

He was now 62 years of age and still very active. He adapted to any necessary changes very quickly and directed his energies to interests he had always cherished, but to which he felt he had never given sufficient time. These were his home and family and public service as represented by his work on the County Council. He interested himself in the larger schemes that the County embarked upon, and more importantly how he could best serve his friends, the constituents. What facilities were needed in the area and how best they could be obtained?

The last County Election took place in 1939 when Billy Newman was elected for Eastry South. He was the first Labour candidate to gain a seat on the Kent County Council. In September 1939 a state of war existed with Germany and elections were suspended for the duration of that war. It was not till 1945 that the next Parliamentary Elections took place. County Council Elections were again held in 1946. There was a great swing towards Labour, but in the Kent County Council Election the Conservatives won enough seats to give them a very substantial majority.

Labour did very well increasing their numbers from one solitary member to some twenty in the new Council.

There were some vacancies on the Aldermanic Bench which needed to be filled and only County Councillors were allowed to participate and vote. Billy Newman was proposed as a Labour candidate alongside a number of Conservatives. It was felt that he stood very little chance against the Conservative nominees with their large majority. However fate does at times move in mysterious and unexpected ways. This was one such occasion.

There were three vacancies on the Aldermanic Bench. Councillor Newman, a Labour candidate, and some five Conservatives were nominated. Two seats were taken by the Conservative nominees with clear majorities, but for the third seat, a number of Conservative Councillors broke ranks and voted for the Labour candidate, Mr William Newman. To the surprise of most present, including members of his own party, he was elected and duly took the third seat. He thus became the first Labour Councillor to be made an Alderman of the Kent County Council.

A number of the conservatives who voted for Councillor Newman did so out of respect for the man and in recognition of his work on the Council. On his way out of the meeting two Conservative Councillors came up and congratulated Mr Newman, and one said, "You may not remember me Billy, but some years ago before you ever came on the Council one of my friends was having difficulties with an insurance company and I was told by a mine Manager to get in touch with a Mr Billy Newman who had a great deal of experience in such matters. He might be able to help you, which you did and as a result the case was successfully resolved. That was many years ago, and much water has passed down the river since then. Well, you may belong to a different Party, but in all you do you're the same man now as you was then. Congratulations! You have earned it!"

In spite of the Conservatives having a large majority on the Kent County Council, they had a great respect for William Newman and during his time on the County Council he was four times re-elected as an Alderman. Elected in 1946, he served continuously as an Alderman for 20 years, until 1967, when at the age of 82, due to ill health, he felt he could no longer carry out duties, which he regarded as essential, he retired from his position on the Kent County Council.

Earlier Billy Newman had served on various Committees of the County Council and had given them his full attention. He made them his centres of interest and activity. At one time whilst he was serving on the Kent Education Committee, he was appointed Chairman of the Dover Divisional Education Authority, serving in that position for many years. The Executive Officers that served the Committee included Dr Corbett and later Mr Hewlett, MA, and then Mr Powell.

Billy Newman, Alderman, attending a Kent County Council Meeting, 1947

He was fortunate to have a strong team of eminent local people on the Committee to give him support. They included Alderman Goodfellow, Cannon Ewart-Roberts of St Mary's Parish Church, County Councillor John Lawton of Deal and Mr Bradley, Chairman of Governors at the Grammar Schools. They were an impressive group of people who served the Schools of Dover District well.

There were several occasions which stand out in my memory. The most controversial moment occurred when the Labour government introduced their proposals to introduce comprehensive education. Mr Hewlett the Dover Divisional Education Officer did a great deal of behind the scenes groundwork. He managed to get agreement of the headteachers of the Secondary Schools to a plan which involved the re-structuring of secondary education in the Dover area.

Prior to the election of the Labour government, a local meeting was organised by Tam Dyall on behalf of the Labour Party. The visiting guest was to be Dick Crossman, the then Shadow Education Minister, a Cambridge academic and a brilliant and persuasive public speaker. The headteachers and many of the teaching staff turned up regardless of political affiliation. It proved a most interesting meeting, with a lively exchange of ideas. It was a full house with between 50 and 100 in attendance at Webb's Hotel where the idea of introducing a comprehensive system in the Dover Area was launched. It was at that moment a great success.

Tony Crosland, a former Oxford Don, became Minister of Education in the Labour goverment and was an enthusiastic supporter of comprehensive education. He issued a Circular, known as 1066, outlining proposals for the implementation of comprehensive structures in various areas of the country. Dover Division got off to an early start with proposals to enable all secondary schools to accept a full intake across the whole range of ability, aged 11 to16. The students would at 16 go forward to a 6th Form College to be established at the Dover Grammar Schools. This proposal caused a great deal of altercation between the members of the Kent County Council and members of the Dover Divisional Executive. The County had their own plans for what was called a Three Tier System and wanted to establish this system throughout Kent. In some parts of the county there was outright opposition to any change to a comprehensive structure, particularly if this meant the closure of Grammar Schools.

Representatives of the Kent Education Committee with the County Education Officer toured the county. A public meeting was organised in Dover and held at the Girls Grammar School. Mr Hewlett MA, wanted Alderman Newman to take the chair, but Mr Haines MA, the County Education Officer insisted that Brigadier McGregor, Chairman of the Kent Education Committee take the Chair.

After some twenty minutes discussion, and hard negotiation concerning the procedures to be followed at the meeting, it was agreed that Brigadier McGregor be appointed Chairman of the meeting with Alderman Newman as Vice-Chairman, and the meeting proceeded. It was a full house. The school hall was packed.

The differing proposals were put with force and clarity and many of those attending the meeting joined in the debate. The vast number at the meeting still preferred the Dover Plan. The County Officials assured the meeting that the Minister would not accept proposals which included a 6th Form College. However, we learned some days later that the Minister, Tony Crossland, had not rejected the Dover Plan. He assured us personally, in a private conversation, that he had not seen the Dover Plan, let alone acted on it and he would receive any proposals sympathetically. I was the person to whom he gave that assurance.

It appears as though it was being held up at County, or by the Ministry Officials at the request of County. The County Secretary of the National Union of Teachers, Mr Baker, was in full agreement with Mr Haines, the County Education Officer, in his opposition to the Dover Plan.

At about this time, before any action could be taken relating to Dover, Tony Crossland was transferred from the Education

Department and moved to the Foreign Office, where he took on the role of Foreign Secretary. He was replaced at the Ministry of Education by Shirley Williams who continued with the comprehensive programme, but followed a different order of prioritisation and implementation of the programme. Those parts of Kent that had decided to follow the County Plan, of having a Three Tier System of Secondary Education, were given the go-ahead. Those areas of Kent which opposed the County Scheme, were allowed to carry on as before, retaining their existing selective system. Dover was one such area, and still remains so.

The watershed in 20th century British politics occurred in 1945 with the election of a Labour government with a mandate for change. Equal opportunity, health for all, and the acceptance that it was our moral obligation to look after the most vulnerable in society. These were all outlined in the Beveridge Report.

The opinion of the government, being guided by its Socialist principles, was that the industrial levers of power should be publicly owned and production should be for the nation. The coal mines, the steel works and road and rail transport were nationalised.

Chapter 62

Change in Public Attitudes. Churchill re-elected.

The three important factors that hindered the implementation of this ambitious programme were; the debts we owed to America, as a result of buying equipment from them during the War, the cost and upkeep of the Empire, and questions of defence as affected by the creation of the atomic bomb. But perhaps the most important feature which all too quickly began to affect post war public opinion was the regime of austerity which people had willingly accepted during the war, but now felt little obligation to continue.

Many people felt they now deserved some "goodies", and were unwilling to wait any longer. After five years with support in the country falling, the Prime Minister, Mr Clement Attlee resigned in 1951. Those serving in the Labour government were tired men. They had served their country well. Attlee, Bevin, Morrison, Cripps had served throughout the war in Churchill's Wartime Coalition government and then over the next 5 years in Attlee's Labour Administration. "They had worked on the greatest programme of peace-time legislation ever considered by the British Parliament." Some of these Ministers were close to exhaustion. The Conservatives, with Mr Churchill as Prime Minister, were returned to Office in 1951 with a very different policy and programme.

Despite many disappointments in the way the Socialist programmes were implemented, Billy Newman remained loyal to the Labour Party, and worked hard in support of the Party, wherever he could. It was not long after the Labour government gained office in 1945 that he was called on for his active support to help the Party at the Gravesend by-election.

This he did with imagination and energy.

This was the first test of continued public support for the Attlee government during the early years of the Administration and it proved positive. The public, it appeared, approved overwhelmingly of the legislative programme, particularly those measures relating to recommendations in the Beveridge Report. The National Health Service is still in existence after some 60 years, and the name of Aneurin Bevan still well remembered.

Billy Newman, whilst appreciating that the outcome for Labour was a great breakthrough in 1945, nevertheless, being the shrewd and experienced politician, realised that to retain the political momentum it would be necessary to keep up the pressure, keep campaigning, fight for those things you believed in. People could soon change their opinions and go back to the old ways. Thus it was that he, with other members of the Labour Party, would be seen out on the door-step, or speaking at public meetings in village and town.

Chapter 63

Elections Since 1945.
Mr Thomas and David Ennals.

The Labour candidate, Mr Thomas was elected as Member of Parliament in 1945. The Labour Mayor of Dover, Mr Goodfellow, oversaw a great deal of good work in the Town, with the rehousing of many of the people of Dover affected by the war. A whole area which became known as Buckland Estate was developed as a housing estate. In order to speed up the rehousing of many of the people in greatest need, pre-fabricated houses were constructed.

Mr Thomas was the first Labour candidate to be elected as Member of Parliament for Dover in 1945. He served in that position until 1950 when the Conservative Major Arbuthnot took back the seat. Major Arbuthnot was the Conservative candidate. He remained the representative for Dover from 1950 until he was defeated by David Ennals for Labour in 1964.

Billy Newman had resigned his position as Secretary of the Tilmanstone Miners Union, but he retained a great deal of his influence with the men at the pits. He devoted the greater part of his time to his County Council work and to the promotion of the Labour Party.

Whilst on the County Council Billy Newman served on various Committees including those of Education. He was Chairman of the Dover Divisional Education Authority for many years and spent a great deal of time fighting for the best possible facilities to be provided for the schools in the Dover area. He was of the belief that all schools should be of equal status and none should be accorded a privileged position, and that the pursuit of excellence be central to any activities undertaken.

Billy Newman fought for improved facilities for older people who found it necessary to reside in County provided

Care Homes. It came to his attention that many people were catered for in old "Work-Houses", which were not conducive to a reasonable life. Eventually and after much effort he persuaded the Kent County Council to open a new building in pleasant grounds with facilities that provided both dignity and a degree of comfort to the residents. This new residence for older people was situated near Broadstairs and the Health Committee paid tribute to Alderman Newman by naming the building "The Newmans".

Chapter 64

International Affairs. World Government. The Spirit of Hope.

His interests were wide and varied, all pertaining to the public good. It included his active support in international affairs. This is illustrated by his work with the movement for "World Government" supported by many people in countries throughout the world as a result of the terrible suffering endured as a consequence of the war. Generations of young men dead. Explosives, bombs rained down on defenceless people. Women and children, whole families burned alive in "Fire-storms". Large swathes of Russia and Germany reduced to ashes... War had become Total War. The indiscriminate killing of civilians had become justified in the eyes of the civilised world. This was the greatest tragedy. Lost were the Christian values of love and compassion.

It took some very brave people to stand up and tell it as it was. Perhaps the best known to continually press his case in the newspapers, in the House of Lords, and in the Church, was my father's friend, The Rev George Bell, the Bishop of Chichester. He, with his close circle of friends including the publisher Victor Gollancz and in Germany, Dietrich Boenhoffer, later executed by the Nazis, kept the spirit of hope alive.

The war ended. Indeed it was in many respects a great victory. There was now a chance to build an enduring peace in a just world. Men of good conscience came together with the aim of building such a world.

The end of one conflict however gave rise to further problems, especially with the successful manufacture of the atomic bomb. There was a struggle for dominance among the victorious Powers. China and India in the East had their own internal problems. However America was deeply entrenched in Europe and determined to ensure that the Communists regimes in Europe be quelled, particularly in France, Italy and Germany. The Russians had made great inroads into Eastern Europe and they too were determined to hold their ground, and that the regimes in those countries they occupied should follow the pattern of Soviet Russia and be Communist States.

These countries with their opposing ideologies and their tremendous power in terms of both natural and technological resources, resulted in a power conflict, the like of which the world had never witnessed. As Oppenheimer restated at the time of the exploding of the atom bomb, that famous phrase, "I am the destroyer of worlds!", and it came close to that.

Such movements as 'Ban the Bomb' attracted large numbers of people right across the social spectrum to demonstrate openly for unilateral disarmament. The Labour Party almost tore itself apart with internal struggles which included Hugh Gaitskell's famous words at the Labour Party Conference, "I will fight, fight and fight again for the soul of the Party I love!"

Demonstrations carried on over a number of years, but with governments firmly against any such protests, people grew tired and the protests became little more than gestures. Thus it was that there was decreasing active support for movements such as the "Crusade for World Government". Those who thoroughly believed in their cause kept up the fight, but most of the public felt it was a "Step too far" in this greatly troubled world.

Though very pragmatic in his every day affairs my father still had his dreams. He would say, "Keep your beliefs, retain your principles and look for the real possibilities that may exist. It is no use keeping your thoughts hidden away. You must have the courage of your convictions and stick your head above the parapet. You must be prepared to suffer ridicule even from those you think of as friends.

"Make clear your arguments. Good examples of your proposition and sound reasons for your case can be most appealing. No longer dreams, we must seek out practical possibilities, backed up by people with that long held yearning, that we work together and help one another."

He had seen it, heard it expressed by leaders of Nations, and then there was the formation of The League of Nations. There was a universal outcry against Italy in the thirties when Mussolini's armies so cruelly conquered Abysinia and again some years later when the Nazis and Fascists joined Franco in the Spanish Civil War. The Italian and German Warplanes bombed the unprotected cities of Spain. They were defenceless and provided easy targets. It was deliberate terror warfare. It was the shape of things to come. And in faraway China, on the other side of the World, very similar things were happening. The brutal Japanese armies brought death and destruction to vast numbers of a peaceful population. There was the invasion of Manchuria followed by further incursions into the heart of China and the cruel burning of vast areas of the city of Nanking and the decimation of its population. The story is well told by Snow in a book circulated by Gollancz and the Left Wing Book Club.

These events took place during the 1930s and deeply influenced my father's mind that we should strive to build a world where there would be no more war. He was no pacifist, but the ultimate aim was not for power but for peace, acknowledging others as equal human beings, deserving of their own space entailing the spirit of Freedom and Respect. "To construct structures involving procedures which ensured such space, procedures that guaranteed the exercise of individual freedom, this was the basis of my father's idea of Socialism."

Part 4

The Close

Me and my father, he scribbled on the back:

The mice at play, when the gaffer is away

Chapter 65

And So to the Close and the End of the Day.

As Winter Comes and Last Leaves Fall,
The Moon full Bright,
A Gentle Light,
So Moves the Day into the Night.

Billy Newman enjoyed his family life with his wife, Margaret, their three daughters and three sons. He kept up his public and political activities till well into his 80s, He was fortunate in that his circle of friends maintained regular contact and they together kept up with all the latest events. Of the comments which he held dear, perhaps his favourite was expressed by Miss Jan MacDonald on friendship.

"Friendship is the Rock, It is the Basis of Hope".
Besides having a pragmatic insight of what could be done, he retained that sense of vision filled with the wonderful possibilities that we as a human race might achieve.

Whatever circumstances might prevail he would say, as he looked out across the sea with all its brilliance, on a bright summer's day:

"Son!
Son! There's a Future Out There!".
Something marvellous!
Something great!"

I felt that summed up his life. "There's a future out! There's a future out there!"

And "As long as there's Hope, the Light will Shine!"

And eyes, bright with optimism, he would say "Together, we will succeed. We will succeed!"

Thank you for letting us share Your Wonderful Journey.

Jean and Bill Newman.

A letter from Mr D. T. Jenkins, J.P.
19 Broadfield Road,
Folkestone.
11th of March 1972.

An Obituary

Former Alderman of the Kent County Council, Mr William Newman of Sandwich Road, Eythorne died on Friday 3rd March aged 88 years. The funeral service, attended by many of his dear friends from all parts of the county, took place on Tuesday at Eythorne Parish Church.

Alderman William Newman JP was a working miner all his life. He entered the pits as a boy of 13 in Yorkshire and came to Kent in 1917. He began work at Tilmanstone Colliery in August of that year and became Secretary of the Tilmanstone Branch of the Kent Mineworkers Association in 1918, a post he held until 1946. He was President of the Kent Mineworkers Association from 1921 to 1933.

He was instrumental in successfully negotiating the first Wages Agreement for Tilmanstone Colliery, and afterwards the first District Wages Agreement for the combined Kent Coalfield. It speaks well for his leadership that whilst being instrumental in getting for the workers of Tilmanstone Colliery the highest wages paid in the Kent Coalfield and thereby achieving the highest output per man shift, only one days stoppage occurred through strikes from 1921 to 1946.

In May 1938, Mr Newman was elected to the Kent County Council and in November 1946 became the first Labour Councillor to be elected to the Aldermanic Bench and continued to be elected as such until at the age of 82, failing health necessitated his giving up of his public duties. An achievement which gave him much pride in his later years was the establishment of "Newman Homes" for the elderly at Broadstairs.

Besides serving as Chairman of the South-Eastern Region, National Assistance Board, he was for many years Chairman of the Dover Divisional Education Executive.

Mr Newman was appointed a Justice of the Peace in 1930 and at the time of his retirement in 1959 was the longest serving Justice on the Wingham Bench

His whole life was spent in the service of his fellow men. The character of the man is best summed up in the words of Mr Frank Rose, Chairman of the Wingham Bench, when referring to the first time he met Mr Newman as an election opponent said, "I lost an election but I gained a life-long friend".

Mr Newman had a staunch faith in his convictions, but these were set in a context of sympathy, which allowed no bitterness, and it could truly be said that he served and was serving his fellow men, and from that service there was no retiring age. He died as he had lived.

D.T. Jenkins. J.P.

For many years Mr David Jenkins was the Director of Finance, representing the management at Tilmanstone Colliery, where he found himself as the main opponent whom Mr Newman faced when disputes occurred relating to questions of wages and Finance. Mr Jenkins represented the owners and management, and was a staunch Conservative

Billy Newman
1884 - 1972

Books on my Fathers' Shelf.

G.D.H. Cole and Raymond Postgate, *The Common People.*
1746-1938. Methuen and Co. References: The War Years
pages 491; Revolution and the Dole pages 531; The Sankey
Commision. 536; Margaret Bondfield 555-575.

Beatrice Webb, *Diaries 1912-1924.* References: Low state of
Civilisation page 188; Robert Smillie Page 197; Black Friday
207; Union Leaders Unfit to Govern. 208-9.

Sidney Webb, *History of Trade Unionism.*

Tom Paine, *Rights of Man.*

R.H. Tawney, *Acquisitive Society.*

Wal Hannington, *The Problem of Depressed Areas.*

John Newsome, *Out of the Pit.* Dedicated to Sir Wyndham
Deedes.

Dr. George Bell, *Biography.* References: 135 and 291.

Bill Deede, *Autobiography.* Pages 351.

Karl Marx, *Das Capital* Vol. 1.

Beverley Nichol, *Cry Havoc.* 1936.
  "Cry Havoc, and let slip the dogs of war."